"This is a splendid guide for those who wish to become acquainted with many of the hundreds of lakes in Yellowstone National Park, whether those accessible by vehicle or by foot. Many of the Park's lakes are barren of sport fish, and anglers will be delighted to learn which of those described contain trout or grayling. Although the author concentrates on the most accessible waters, there are suggestions for more demanding and adventuresome explorations."

— **Nelson Bryant, Outdoors Columnist,
THE NEW YORK TIMES**

"The lakes of Yellowstone back country are its magnets, and the magnetic field — the wilderness of Yellowstone — is some of the best. This is the kind of guide based on foot-slogging and toil that is truly useful. The author's suggestions reflect his experience in hints about weather, distances, trail difficulty. Historical notes and place-name information are a bonus. I'd recommend it."

— **Rick Graetz, Publisher,
MONTANA MAGAZINE**

"An invaluable guidebook to someone like myself who has a limited amount of time and wants to make the most of it. Thanks to Steve Pierce, I can find six species of sport fish in some of the most scenic lakes in the USA, most of them just a day-hike away."

— **Steve Kanaly, "Dallas" co-star
and avid fisherman**

"Steve Pierce has produced a unique guide to the lakes of our first — and some say greatest — national park. From gigantic Yellowstone Lake, drained by the nation's longest free-flowing river, to small backcountry lakes with wonderful names like Wyodaho, Crevice, Geode, and Dewdrop, there's useful information here for day-hikers and backpackers alike."

— **Jonathan F. King, Managing Editor,
SIERRA**

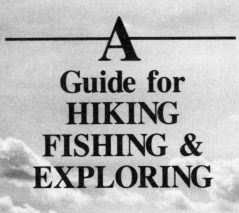

# A
## Guide for
## HIKING
## FISHING &
## EXPLORING

# The LAKES of

THE MOUNTAINEERS

Seattle

# YELLOWSTONE

## Steve Pierce

**The Mountaineers: Organized 1906**

" . . .to explore, study, preserve, and enjoy the natural beauty of
the Northwest."

© 1987 by Steve Pierce
All rights reserved

Published by The Mountaineers
306 2nd Avenue West, Seattle, Washington, 98119

Published simultaneously in Canada by Douglas & McIntyre Ltd.
1615 Venables Street, Vancouver, B. C. V5L 2H1

Manufactured in the United States of America

Edited by Connie Bourassa-Shaw
Cover design by Elizabeth Watson
Book design by Bridget Culligan
Maps by Denise Zaremba Bauman

Photos: Cover—Cascade Lake, with yellow-headed blackbird inset, by
Steve Pierce. Back cover inset © Tom Montgomery.
All interior photos by the author.
Title photo—Yellowstone Lake's Southeast Arm

Library of Congress Cataloging in Publication Data
Pierce, Steve, 1941–
The lakes of Yellowstone.

Includes index.
1. Outdoor recreation—Yellowstone National Park—
Guide-books. 2. Hiking—Yellowstone National Park—
Guide-books. 3. Fishing—Yellowstone National Park—
Guide-books. 4. Backpacking—Yellowstone National Park—
Guide-books. 5. Yellowstone National Park—Guide-books.
I. Title.
GV191.42.Y44P54  1987       917.87'52       87-5583
ISBN 0-89886-139-X

*Dedicated with love
to the memory of my dad*
H. A. (Guy) Pierce

*Douglas fir cones*

# Contents

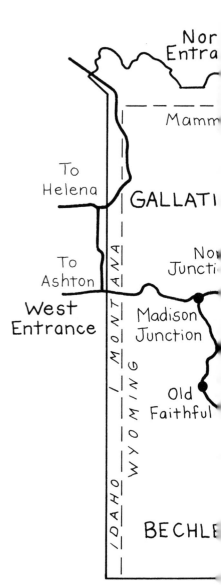

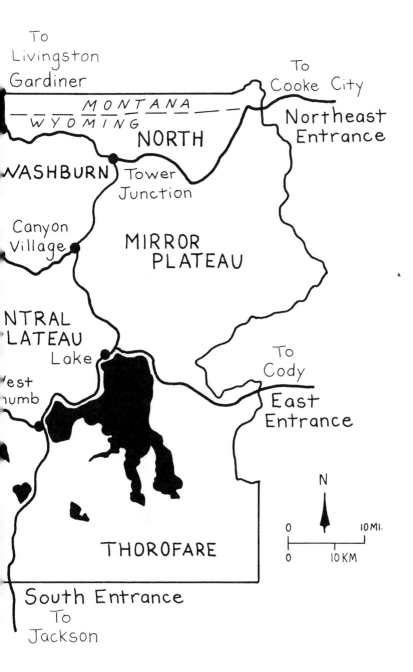

*Beula Lake Trail*

# Preface

The purpose of this book is to provide useful and factual information about the lakes in Yellowstone National Park. Originally, the idea of writing a guidebook about Yellowstone's lakes was the farthest thing from my mind. However, during the time I spent researching the lakes, I spoke with people who wanted to know where a particular lake was located, how difficult it was to reach, what it was like and if it contained fish. I saw countless very determined and, oftentimes, frustrated people fishing in lakes that are naturally barren. As my research continued it became evident that *The Lakes of Yellowstone* had to be a guidebook. It had to be written for the hiker, backpacker and fisherman who is interested in a lake's location, distance, access, environment, wildlife, fishing, thermal features and history. *The Lakes of Yellowstone* is written with the sincere hope that the users of this book will find information that will make their Yellowstone visit a bit more enjoyable.

Of the hundreds of lakes in Yellowstone, the lakes featured in this book are the ones that are among the most accessible and most visited; they are, for the most part, the roadside lakes and the lakes reached by a reasonable day hike, up to 5 miles one way. Although these lakes receive their fair share of backpackers and backcountry campers, most are visited by day hikers.

In addition to the lakes with complete descriptions, this book offers just enough information on some other lakes to appeal to those of you who like to explore on your own. The lack of a detailed description or, is some cases, even a trail, may actually make your exploration of that lake more intriguing and most certainly, will offer you a greater degree of solitude.

Much of the information in this book came from official Yellowstone records. The Fish and Wildlife Service prepares Annual Project Reports of the Fishery and Aquatic Management Program in Yellowstone National Park. At the request of the National Park Service, the Fish and Wildlife Service

*Cascade Lake*

has, for more than 20 years, undertaken the painstaking and time-consuming process of surveying and recording the physical, chemical and biological characteristics of Yellowstone's aquatic resources. These characteristics include the size and depth of lakes, a listing of the lakes that contain sport fish and the lakes' fish stocking history. Many of the park lakes are unsurveyed and a few of the lakes in this book, where size or depth is still unknown, have only been partially surveyed or not surveyed at all.

Information concerning how particular lakes were named came from a 1935 report called *Place Names of Yellowstone National Park*, compiled by C. Max Bauer, a park naturalist.

# Acknowledgments

It would not be possible to write a book such as this without the help and cooperation of many people. I want to thank all of those who shared their thoughts and knowledge with me, provided helpful advice and, at times, much needed criticism. All of you are a part of this book. I especially want to thank a few contributors.

My wife Marilyn edited the book and gave me the support and confidence that I needed. My daugher Lynn's quiet and considerate, but constant, interruptions while I wrote helped me to maintain a perspective as to the needs of my family. My son Steve, with his friend, Leslie Lister, joined me in Yellowstone on the trip to Shoshone Lake and provided me with wonderful memories of a father and son adventure.

My lifelong friend Steve Haase endured 7 miles of canoeing on Shoshone Lake one cold, windy, sleet-filled morning. My brother-in-law Mack Lee shared time with me in Yellowstone and went with me to Beula and Hering lakes.

Bob Gresswell, a Fish and Wildlife Service biologist, personally gathered much of the technical and statistical data recorded in Yellowstone's Aquatic Survey Reports, read the manuscript for accuracy and answered my questions day and night for more than 18 months. Dan Carty, another Fish and Wildlife Service biologist, shared hours with me discussing the waters and fish of Yellowstone, showed me the backcountry areas of Yellowstone Lake and shared his home with me. Ron Jones, project leader of the Fisheries Management Division in Yellowstone, permitted me access to the Annual Project Reports of the Fishery and Aquatic Management Programs. Crystal Hudson helped me with research for facts and historical information; John Varley provided most of the fish stocking history; Rick Hutchinson aided me with the geological history of Yellowstone; and Gary Brown, Greg Kroll, Marji Siring, Marily Nixon, Tom Olliff, Mark Marschall, Lee Whitlesea and Chris Sobieski gave me their valuable help and assistance.

*Shoshone Lake*

Cecil C. Hoge, Jr., president of Sea Eagle, provided me with 300X inflatable canoes.

And, finally, my thanks to Annie, a very special friend, who—not realizing it—helped and inspired me when she said, at just the right time, "You ought to write a book!"

*Author making notes at Grebe Lake*

*Footbridge across Firehole River, Mallard Lake Trail*

# Introduction

There are hundreds of lakes within the 3472 square miles of Yellowstone National Park. Many are small lakes and ponds from just barely an acre up to 35 or 40 acres. Some are large expanses of open water, like Yellowstone Lake, which measures 87,450 acres. Shoshone Lake, 8050 acres, is the largest backcountry lake in the lower 48 states. There is no road access to Shoshone; it can be reached only by hiking or canoeing. Many of the lakes in Yellowstone lie alongside the highway or are near enough to the road that they are easily accessible. Others can be reached by a short day hike of ½ to 3 miles. Many lakes are on well-defined trails through open meadows and lodgepole pine forests. Some require backpacking on overnight trips of up to 8 or 9 miles one way. Overall, Yellowstone contains more lakes that are truly wild—beautiful backcountry wilderness lakes with closer and easier access—than any other part of the country.

A visit to Yellowstone's lakes offers excellent opportunities to see a variety of wildlife. At backcountry lakes you can see

*South Twin Lake*

wildlife such as beaver, otter, loons, osprey and eagles that you will not normally see from the road. You can still see deer, elk, moose, buffalo and even bears in the park. (Your chances of seeing a bear in the backcountry are much better than from the road. Bears are shy and secretive creatures that prefer the solitude and tranquil environment of the back- country to the noise and crowds of the highways and the pop- ulated areas of Yellowstone.) Not only will you see more variety of wildlife at these backcountry lakes, you will see them in a more natural state.

If you have ever fished in one of Yellowstone's lakes with- out catching fish, having a strike or even seeing a rise, don't feel bad. That experience has happened time and again and will continue to happen, because more than half of Yellow- stone's lakes are naturally barren. Cutthroat trout were among the first species of fish to enter Yellowstone. They migrated, thousands of years ago, into the Yellowstone region from the Snake River and Atlantic Creek over Two Ocean Pass, south of Yellowstone, and into the Yellowstone River. As they migrated into the area that is now Yellowstone Na- tional Park, they inhabited the waters of the Yellowstone River drainage, an area that encompasses more than half of the park.

In 1890, when stocking of fish began in Yellowstone, almost every brook, stream, river, lake, pothole and pond was stocked—with little knowledge as to whether the fish could survive. In many cases they did not. Their demise was due mainly to a lack of spawning habitat and to winterkill.

If the water chemistry, temperature and availability of food in a lake is sufficient to support fish life, there must also be a proper environment for fish to reproduce. Trout will occa- sionally move into outlet streams to spawn, but, of inlets and outlets, the inlet stream is more important. Trout seem to prefer to migrate upstream to a narrow section of smooth flowing water and deposit their eggs in shallow redds (nests) they have dug into the gravel of the stream bottom. If this environment does not exist and a lake is without proper spawning habitat, fish that have been planted in a lake will not reproduce, and eventually their population will dwindle until the lake returns to its original barren state.

*Above: Mule deer. Below: Moose at Obsidian Creek*

Winterkill results when a shallow lake with an insufficient inflow of water holding dissolved oxygen freezes over. Because of the ice cover, the lake can't absorb oxygen from the air and the dissolved oxygen content of the water becomes so low that the fish suffocate. Many of Yellowstone's lakes are shallow and lack the inflow of water that would enable fish to survive.

Yellowstone's lakes offer adventure, excitement, serenity and the chance to experience a pristine part of nature the way it existed when Yellowstone was explored by the first white man, John Colter, in 1807. Lakes in some areas of Yellowstone are rarely visited. Some have no direct trail access, others have no fish. A lake without fish usually means a lake without people and these are among the most enjoyable lakes to visit. The whisper of a forest breeze, singing birds or maybe the cry of a loon are the only sounds you are likely to hear. Visiting these lakes is a unique wilderness experience because you will not only enjoy a personal relationship with nature, wild and primordial, but simply because the lakes are beautiful, peaceful places to be.

## DAY HIKES AND BACKCOUNTRY USE

Most of Yellowstone, in fact about 99 percent, lies beyond the 300 miles of roads in the park; it is the backcountry. What constitutes "backcountry" is a matter of personal opinion. To some it may mean being far enough from the road that you can no longer see the road. To others it might mean being 10 miles or more from the nearest road. In Yellowstone it takes little more than venturing far enough away from the sights and sounds of other tourists and passing cars to feel the dawnlike freshness of the wilderness that surrounds you. There are few places on this continent where you will find such a unique combination of wilderness, beautiful scenery, abundant wildlife and countless natural wonders in one concentrated area. Yellowstone's backcountry, although explored and visited for decades, remains a pristine wilderness.

There are a few things you should know and consider before going into the backcountry, whether it is for a short day hike or an overnight backpacking trip. It is always a good idea to

*Ice Lake Trailhead*

check with the backcountry office in that region of the park you plan to visit. You will get helpful advice on weather, trail conditions and any bear activity that might be in the area. Sometimes, due to unusual bear activity, certain areas are temporarily closed to travel or restricted to parties of 4 or more. It's worth taking the time to know as much as you can about the area you are going to be hiking or backpacking in.

If you are going on an overnight trip, a backcountry permit is required. You can get one free at any ranger station or backcountry office. As overnight camping in the backcountry is allowed only at designated campsites, the permit reserves the site for you and also lets the area ranger know when you are going, the route you are taking and how long you plan to stay. Just in case you should get into some kind of trouble, it is comforting to know that someone knows where you are and how long you are going to be there. The permit system also keeps backcountry areas from becoming overcrowded and limits overnight backcountry use to the number of campsites in a particular area.

*Black bear*

If you are going on a day hike (going and returning on the same day), a backcountry permit is not required. Rather than just taking off with only the clothes on your back and a fishing rod in hand, you should carry a few essential items in a daypack.

Necessary items are:

Rainsuit or poncho—It can rain anytime in the mountains.

Light coat or sweater—At these elevations, even in the summer, it can get cold in a hurry.

Extra clothes—Just in case you should get wet.

Hat—Keeps your head dry and prevents heat loss.

Sunglasses—Especially necessary when hiking on very bright days.

Water—A light plastic container to carry at least 1 quart.

Matches—Waterproof, in a waterproof container.

Firestarter—Easy and fast if you have to build a fire.

Food—Pack a lunch and be sure to include snacks such as candy and fruit.

Extra food—It is always a good idea to have a little more than you want or actually need.

First-aid kit—Start with a small, basic kit, then add anything that might apply to your personal needs.

Insect repellent—Buy the best you can find; the mosquitoes can be treacherous.

Knife—Always handy and sometimes needed.

Compass and topographic map—These will help you find your way and identify landmarks.

Flashlight—Carry one that is small and lightweight, just in case you haven't returned by dark.

Whistle—If you do get into trouble or get lost, it takes much less effort to blow a whistle than it does to yell. Whistles are also louder.

Fishing gear and permit—If you are going to fish.

You can certainly add your own items—such as a camera or guidebook—to the list. The idea is to take only what you need and not end up with a pack so heavy and uncomfortable that it takes away from the pleasure of hiking in the backcountry. Your daypack should weigh no more than 12 to 15 pounds.

## FISHING

Yellowstone is considered to have the best trout fishing in the United States, with the exception of Alaska. It probably does. There are, of course, other areas of the country that have great fishing, but these are limited to some specific lake or stream—you still have to travel long distances to get from one good fishery to another. Due to the dedication, research and hard work of the National Park Service and the Fish and Wildlife Service biologists and biological aids in Yellowstone, you will find, in one concentrated area, an outstanding collection of waters. The objective of the National Park Service is to manage the park fisheries as an essential part of the park ecosystem by preserving and restoring native species of fish, by making fish available to the animals that need them for survival and by providing quality fishing for park visitors.

The fishing season in Yellowstone opens the latter part of May for most of the park. Some areas are not open to fishing until mid-June, others open as late as mid-July. To complicate matters, some waters are permanently closed to fishing, and catch limits vary from place to place. Although some waters are catch and release only, this practice is encouraged throughout the park. Be sure to read the fishing regulations for Yellowstone. It is entirely your responsibility to know the rules and regulations concerning the particular waters you are fishing. A non-fee permit is required for anyone 12 and older, and the permit must be in your possession when you are fishing. You can get one by asking for it at any of the entrance stations or at any backcountry office in the park.

The lake you decide to fish in is, of course, a matter of choice. Those along the roads—even the barren ones—are the lakes fished most often by the most people. The reason for this is obvious: all you have to do is stop your car, get out and

*Fishing in Lewis River just below Shoshone Lake*

start fishing. With a little effort, you can find wonderful fishing in a number of lakes that can be reached by a short day hike.

Of the 18 species of fish known in Yellowstone waters, 6 are considered sport fish: grayling, cutthroat, rainbow, brook, brown and lake trout. No lake contains all 6 species. With a few exceptions, most lakes that contain sport fish have only 1 species.

## BOATING

The use of power boats in Yellowstone is restricted to the open waters of Yellowstone and Lewis lakes. The use of hand-propelled boats, such as rafts and canoes, is allowed on some park lakes, but is prohibited on all park rivers and streams except the Lewis River Channel between Lewis and Shoshone lakes. You must obtain a permit and a set of boating regulations at either the Yellowstone Lake Ranger Station or the

Grant Village Ranger Station for the use of any boat, regardless of type and size.

**A WORD OF CAUTION:** Sudden storms and strong southwest winds, which occur almost daily on Yellowstone's large lakes, can create hazardous boating conditions. Hand-propelled craft should stay close to shore at all times and not venture out across these large lakes. A good rule of thumb is: if you capsize and cannot wade ashore, you are too far out. It doesn't matter if you are a strong swimmer. These waters are icy cold and survival time is only a matter of minutes.

## SAFETY IN THE BACKCOUNTRY

When you're in Yellowstone's backcountry, it's rather easy to get caught up in its natural beauty and wonders. There are times and places when it becomes almost impossible not to wander from the trail to admire wildflowers that have the variety and color to boggle the mind. There are countless hydrothermal areas where nature's plumbing system has created a network of geysers, hot springs, mud pots and fumaroles. Wildlife is everywhere.

The important things to know are where you are, where you are going and how you can get back to where you started. With the use of a topographic map, you can also know what to expect in the terrain where you will be hiking. Knowing where you are in the backcountry and that you can get out safely is a serious matter. There's not much problem in hiking from the trailhead to point A, turning around and hiking back to the trailhead. On the other hand, if you're hiking or backpacking through a series of trail junctions and off-trail travel, a compass and topographic map are indispensable items. As your compass will point you in the right direction, a topo, when properly positioned, will show the location of lakes, streams, woods, meadows, marshes and mountain peaks. By being able to identify landmarks and the terrain around you, you will know where you are in relation to your destination. If you have to leave a trail to reach a lake, the topo map can help you identify landmarks so that you know where to leave the trail and which direction to go. A 15-minute topo covers an area about 12.5 by 17.5 miles, with 40-foot contour inter-

*Above: Example of thermal area's thin crust.*
*Below: Firehole Lake, one of Yellowstone's large hot pools*

vals. It is always a good idea to study your map before you start out. By pinpointing your location before you leave, you will know what to expect in the terrain that lies ahead.

Backcountry trails are designed and maintained for travel. They were constructed for use and, consequently, show the wear and tear from hikers and backpackers. If you should leave the trail, never go so far away that you lose sight of the trail—unless you are experienced in the backcountry.

To explore thermal areas, walk the shores of a lake or stream or approach a meadow blanketed in wildflowers is part of the wilderness experience. These experiences, however, can have a lasting effect on the land and terrain you are hiking through. If you leave the trail, even for just a short distance, tread lightly and be aware of where you are walking and what you are walking on. You can leave scars on the land that might last for years. You can add to or create erosion just by leaving the trail to take a more direct route to your destination or to explore some area or thing that is of interest to you.

When you unexpectedly come upon a thermal area in the backcountry, it can be interesting and exciting. It can also be

*Antelope*

quite dangerous! Approach thermal areas with extreme caution. What appears to be solid ground around these areas is sometimes only a thin crusty layer of mineral deposits that can break and open up under your weight. It's not uncommon to see the bleached bones of an animal that wandered too close to a hot spring where the thin crust gave way. There are some areas in the backcountry where you might find tiny, delicate thermal features that are beautiful and amazing to observe. They can be quite fragile, and hikers who pick, peck, and prod at the features can, in a few seconds, destroy what nature has taken eons to create.

Yellowstone's variety and abundance of wildlife and the ease with which it can be seen are probably the main reasons for going into the backcountry. While wildlife shouldn't be feared, you should show a healthy respect for all animals and maintain a safe distance, especially if there are young present. Getting too close to or, worse, between a mother and her baby is to invite trouble. A wild animal will attack you if it feels you are a threat to its offspring. You should avoid any area where there are nesting birds or waterfowl, particularly swans. They are very easy to disturb and will leave their nests if you approach. Their nest then becomes vulnerable to predation and the success of the hatch becomes questionable.

For many, the Yellowstone experience, especially the backcountry, may be a first-time experience. By simply applying some forethought, using sound judgment and plain old common sense to become familiar with the unfamiliar, to think when knowledge and acquaintance may be lacking, backcountry travel can be a safe, exciting and wonderful adventure. We, like the generations before us, must do our part to preserve and protect this great national estate. When we intrude upon what is wild and natural, it can never again be as wild or as natural as it was. No matter how good our intentions, we upset nature's balance to some degree. Our increasing fondness for and yearning to be a part of the wilderness experience leads us to travel through pristine areas, and we, through our visits, always leave something behind. Each of us, in our own way, must help to maintain, unspoiled and unmarred for future generations, the unique wilderness environment that is Yellowstone.

*Buffalo are commonly seen around Indian Pond*

# Thorofare Region

1 Yellowstone Lake
2 Indian Pond
3 Sylvan Lake
4 Eleanor Lake
5 Riddle Lake

**OTHER LAKES TO EXPLORE**

6 Glade Lake
7 Trail Lake
8 Alder Lake
9 Mariposa Lake
10 Outlet Lake
11 Heart Lake
12 Sheridan Lake
13 Basin Creek Lake
14 Forest Lake
15 Aster Lake
16 Delusion Lake

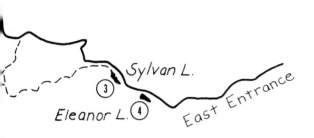

Indian Pond

Sylvan L.

③

Eleanor L. ④

East Entrance

⑥

Glade L.

Southeast Arm

Molly Islands

Thorofare Trail

Trail

Trail L. ⑦

Yellowstone R.

⑨

Mariposa L.

*The Promontory on Yellowstone Lake*

---1---

## Yellowstone Lake

**Location** - On the highway between West Thumb and Fishing Bridge and the East Entrance Highway between Fishing Bridge and Lake Butte

**Access** - On the highway

**USGS topographic maps** - Canyon Village, Wyoming; West Thumb, Wyoming; Frank Island, Wyoming; Eagle Peak, Wyoming

**Size** - 87,450 acres

**Depth** - Average 139 feet, maximum 320 feet

**Elevation** - 7733 feet

**Fish type** - Cutthroat trout

*National Park Service patrol cabin on Peale Island*
*near the tip of Yellowstone Lake's South Arm*

Around 600,000 years ago, a volcanic eruption of enormous proportions occurred in the center of Yellowstone. The top of the volcanic mountain blew away, sending ash and debris throughout much of North America. What remained of the mountain collapsed into the partially emptied magma chambers below, forming an oval or saucer-shaped caldera covering an area of 1000 square miles. Part of this caldera is the 136-square-mile basin of Yellowstone Lake. Originally the lake was 300 feet higher than it is now, extending northward across the Hayden Valley to the base of Mt. Washburn, an area covering over 300 square miles.

When Yellowstone Lake was first formed, covering an area more than twice its present size, it drained into the Pacific Ocean by way of the Snake River. Later, during the formation of the Grand Canyon of the Yellowstone, the lake drained to the north into Hudson Bay. Currently, the lake's only outlet is the Yellowstone River, the longest (671 miles) free-flowing U.S. river, which drains into the Gulf of Mexico through the Missouri River system.

For some time now, the lake basin has been tilting in a northeast to southwest direction, raising the area just north of the lake in the vicinity of Mary Bay and Fishing Bridge. The elevation around the lake's lower end does not drop substantially until LeHardy Rapids, 3 miles downstream from Fishing Bridge. Although the largest stream to enter the lake is the Yellowstone River in the Southeast Arm, an additional 123 tributaries provide water to fill the 12,095,000-acre-feet

*Yellowstone River outlet near Fishing Bridge*

*LeHardy Rapids*

capacity of the lake. Due to the size of the lake basin and rate
of inflow-outflow exchange of water, the water level fluc-
tuates only 4 to 5 feet per year, and it takes almost 10 years to
completely displace all of the water in the lake.

Yellowstone Lake appeared as Lake Eustis on Lewis and
Clark's map of 1814, named for William Eustis, secretary of
war from 1809 to 1812 under President Madison. It was later
called Sublette Lake, for William Sublette, a trapper of the
1820s. Finally, in 1839, trappers and traders of the region
named it Yellowstone Lake.

Perhaps one of the best ways to see the enormous size and
changing nature and disposition of Yellowstone Lake is to see
the lake from the overlook at Lake Butte, 9 miles east of Fishing Bridge and a 1-mile drive off the main highway. From the
Lake Butte overlook you can see most of Yellowstone Lake,
600 feet below, Two Ocean Plateau south of the lake and the
Absaroka Mountains to the east. On an exceptionally clear
day, you can see the Tetons, 70 miles southwest. The view

from Lake Butte at sunset is one of the most beautiful in the park.

The drive around Yellowstone Lake, a little more than 30 miles, can take an hour or it can take all day. You could spend your entire vacation in the park just at Yellowstone Lake. There are thermal features to explore, especially near West Thumb, and turnouts and picnic areas with good views and access to the lakeshore. Almost every species of wildlife in Yellowstone can be found near the lake, and it is the most popular fishery in the park. In addition to the 30 miles of shoreline accessible by car, there are another 80 miles of shoreline accessible by foot or boat. This is the part of the lake, and of Yellowstone Park, that is a world apart from the crowds, traffic jams and populated centers of the park. The far reaches of the lake and remote backcountry are true wilderness, seen and explored each year by only a few of Yellowstone's visitors.

There are 2 trails near the shores of Yellowstone Lake. The Thorofare Trail begins about 9 miles east of Fishing Bridge, on the south side of the East Entrance Highway just west of Lake Butte Drive. Going south, this trail follows the eastern shore of Yellowstone Lake for more than 20 miles to the junction with the Trail Creek Trail below the Southeast Arm of Yellowstone Lake. The Thorofare Trail offers short or long day hikes, as well as extended trips into the secluded backcountry areas of Yellowstone Lake.

The 22-mile Trail Creek Trail is definitely a backcountry trip that requires several days. It connects the Thorofare Trail to the Heart Lake Trail and travels through some of the most beautiful wilderness in Yellowstone, skirting the tip of the South and Southeast arms of Yellowstone Lake. From Trail Creek Trail's junction with the Heart Lake Trail, it is 8 miles to the Heart Lake Trailhead on the South Entrance Road. The total length of the trails around Yellowstone Lake is 50 miles.

Depending on weather conditions, which can be severe and dangerous at times, power boats can reach the Promontory and South or Southeast arms of the lake in a relatively short time. Once in the arms of the lake, however, power boats are restricted to a speed of 5 miles per hour, and the last 2 miles of the arms are closed to power boating and restricted to hand-propelled craft. The last 2 miles of Flat Mountain Arm are also restricted to hand-propelled craft. Boats over 16 feet long must stay at least a quarter mile from the shore of the South or Southeast arms, except to load or unload passengers; and boats are not allowed to approach the Molly Islands in the Southeast Arm because pelicans use the 2 small islands as nesting areas.

Canoeing the far reaches of Yellowstone Lake is a fascinating wilderness experience and a worthwhile and memorable adventure, but several considerations should be made before your trip. Almost daily, beginning by late morning or early afternoon, strong southwest winds occur suddenly and create

*Yellowstone Lake's West Thumb*

large waves and hazardous boating conditions. The currents, which move the surface water from the south and southwest to the north and northeast, combined with strong southwest winds, create waves that commonly reach heights of 5 or 6 feet. These waves are choppy and extremely close together. Many times, canoes—and even large power boats—have capsized, with fatal results. With water temperatures around 55 degrees in summer, survival time is short, even for a boater with a life jacket on. It takes only 10 to 15 minutes to become hypothermic in these frigid waters. By staying close to land, so that you could wade ashore in the event of an emergency, you might prevent an unnecessary and possibly fatal disaster.

Another consideration for your canoe trip is time. Depending on the weather (and you should always plan for the worst), your physical condition and the load you are carrying in your canoe, it could take 2 or even 3 days to get into the arms. With 2 or 3 days to get around the arms and another 2 or 3 to come out, you would spend a hard week, most of it just paddling around the lake. With so much to see and explore in this wilderness, you should allow at least 10 days or 2 weeks for a canoe trip on Yellowstone Lake.

For over a century, since tourists began visiting the area, Yellowstone Lake has experienced more fishing pressure than any other park water. Because of its enormous size and the fact that it holds the largest inland cutthroat trout population in the world, people believed that the supply of native cutthroat was inexhaustible. This was not so.

It was not until 1920 that a daily limit of any kind was set for sportfishing on Yellowstone Lake. The limit was 20 fish per day, any size. Also in 1920, a commercial fishing operation, begun in the late 1800s to provide guests of the Lake Hotel with fresh trout, was halted.

Between 1899 and 1956, 818 million cutthroat trout eggs were harvested from spawners as they entered the lake tributaries. In 1940, 43.5 million eggs were taken. Large quantities of eggs were sent to state game and fish departments and federal hatcheries to become a main source of supply for many of the Western states. Some eggs were kept at a hatchery that had been established at Lake Village and were replanted into Yellowstone Lake and other waters in the park. The hatchery

*Above: Moose grazing along shore of Yellowstone Lake near Lake Lodge. Below: Buffalo near banks of Yellowstone River in Hayden Valley*

*Grand Canyon of the Yellowstone and Lower Falls*

was closed in 1953, after it was determined that trout could adequately sustain themselves through natural reproduction.

The annual wildlife harvest of cutthroat is the principal management objective of the National Park Service: to manage the park fisheries as an integral part of the park ecosystem, making fish available, first and foremost, to the animals that need them for survival. The annual wildlife harvest from Yellowstone Lake—taken by mink, osprey, bald and golden eagles, loons, mergansers, gulls, herons, pelicans and bear—accounts for approximately 500,000 cutthroats. Most of these are taken from the southern portion of the lake and lake tributaries during the trout's spawning runs.

In 1948, with the concern that the trout population had substantially declined, the U.S. Fish and Wildlife Service began its first series of detailed studies on Yellowstone Lake. Common belief held that all waters containing fish produced a surplus that could be harvested yearly and, if that surplus was removed each year, the fishery could be sustained indefinitely. The theory was referred to as "maximum sustained yield" and was widely accepted during the 1940s and 1950s. This didn't take into account, however, the fact that environmental changes could alter the number of trout being reproduced and harvested or the fact that more people were coming to Yellowstone each year. More fishermen were fishing for longer periods of time and catching more fish than any surplus would allow. There was also a lack of reliable feedback to determine the number of fish being harvested annually.

In 1962 the National Park Service gave the Fisheries Management Division of the U.S. Fish and Wildlife Service the responsibility for monitoring the Yellowstone Lake fishery. Although daily limits had been reduced to 3 per day, the catch rate continued to decline and reached an all-time low in 1968. Beginning in 1969, in an effort to halt the continued decline in the trout population, restore those populations to previous levels and provide quality fishing rather than maximum harvest, the Fish and Wildlife Service implemented a series of restrictions and regulations. Bait fishing became illegal in 1969 and in 1970 a 14-inch minimum size limit was set. This new size limit, however, resulted in a decrease in older and larger fish, which reduced the number of spawning fish—a situation not regarded with favor when attempting to increase the total fish population. In 1973 Fishing Bridge was closed to fishing and the daily catch limit was reduced to 2 fish. In an effort to improve the overall size, age and number of spawning trout, a 13-inch maximum size limit was set in 1975 and remains in effect today. These changes seem to have accomplished the overall objective. The current population of cutthroat trout in Yellowstone Lake is close to what it was historically. More and larger fish are being caught and returned to the lake, providing a quality of fishing that hasn't existed for many years.

Even though Yellowstone Lake held an enormous quantity of native cutthroat trout, attempts were made to introduce other species. In 1889 and 1890, a total of 12,000 mountain whitefish were stocked in the Yellowstone River just below the lake. Other plants included rainbow trout: 3000 in 1902 and 3800 in 1907 in the lake, and an unknown number in the river in 1929. Landlocked salmon were also planted in the lake: 7000 in 1908 and 5000 in 1909. All of these plants were unsuccessful, however; no salmon survived and none are present in the lake today. Longnose suckers, longnose dace, lake chubs and redside shiners are some species that did survive. These species were probably introduced to the lake by fishermen, who used them as baitfish, although one, the longnose sucker, may have been part of an official 1923 plant of forage minnows.

When events such as these, which took place over a period of more than 95 years, are lumped together, it might give the impression that a large, magnificent body of water in a wonderful setting like Yellowstone was discovered and that a wild and wanton depletion of a national treasure took place. Nothing could be further from the truth. It is through our imperfections and shortcomings that we are able to learn and profit. Such is the case with Yellowstone Lake. Yellowstone and all that it holds is a national treasure. There will always be disputes over other ways and better ways of managing and maintaining this resource. If it were not for the work and dedication of a handful of people who are managing this resource to the best of their ability, there might not be a fishery in Yellowstone Lake.

# 2

## Indian Pond

**Location** - On the south side of the East Entrance Road, 3.1 miles east of Fishing Bridge

**Access** - Near the highway

**USGS topographic map** - Canyon Village, Wyoming

**Size** - 24 acres

**Depth** - Maximum 72 feet

**Elevation** - 7780 feet

**Fish type** - Cutthroat trout

Indian Pond was so named because the surrounding area was the site of an Indian campground. In 1930 the name was changed to Squaw Lake, until 1980, when it was changed back to its original name. It is still referred to as Squaw Lake on 15- and 30-minute USGS topographic maps. Indian Pond lies near the northwest end of Yellowstone Lake's Mary Bay, in a small crater formed by an ancient hydrothermal explosion. Because of its nearness to Yellowstone Lake, you can al-

*Buffalo*

most always see ducks, geese, pelicans, gulls and a variety of shorebirds there. Buffalo are frequently seen around the lake and in the early morning and late evening, moose are sometimes spotted in the meadow around the trees on the south end between Indian Pond and Yellowstone Lake.

Yellowstone Lake's tributaries were stocked heavily during the early 1900s and, probably, so was Indian Pond. The first official stocking in Indian Pond was 50,000 cutthroat trout in 1923. Additional plants were made in 1925, 1954, 1956 and 1958. During this period, more than 4 million fry and fingerlings were planted in Indian Pond in an effort to maintain a quality fishery.

Small springs feed Indian Pond along the southeast and northwest shores, but the major water source is from underground springs. The outlet drains from the southwest end of the lake into Yellowstone Lake. Although some fish spawning may occur, conditions in the outlet stream are poor and spawning is restricted to a few riffles and pools where suitable bottom types exist. With limited spawning conditions, Indian Pond can sustain only a relatively small fish population. Yellowstone Lake is 50 feet lower than Indian Pond, and the gradient is fairly steep, but there are no barriers to fish migration in the outlet stream that connects Indian Pond with Yellowstone Lake. Since the cutthroat more than likely entered the lake this way, migration probably still occurs during high water periods, and Yellowstone Lake cutthroat mix with Indian Pond cutthroat, thereby sustaining the fish population.

---

# 3
# Sylvan Lake

**Location** - On the south side of the East Entrance Highway, 16.5 miles east of Fishing Bridge, 10.2 miles west of the east entrance

**Access** - On the highway

**USGS topographic map** - Eagle Peak, Wyoming

**Size** - 28 acres

*Sylvan Lake*

**Depth** - Average 7 feet, maximum 21 feet

**Elevation** - 8410 feet

**Fish type** - Cutthroat trout

The word *sylvan* refers to being located in the woods. Sylvan Lake was named by the Hayden Expedition of 1871 because of the dense forest that surrounds the water. The beauty and briskness of this high alpine lake, its cold, clear waters, its tree-covered islands and its views of snowcapped, 10,238-foot Top Notch Peak to the southeast and 9948-foot Grizzly Peak to the south make this, perhaps, the prettiest of all the roadside lakes in Yellowstone. There is a picnic area on the northwest end of the lake and turnouts along the highway, with plenty of room for visitors to park.

There are 2 inlet streams that supply water to the lake. One enters the lake on the northeast side and the other at the southeast end. Both flow through culverts underneath the highway. The outlet stream flows from the west side, just south of midlake, and into nearby Clear Creek. Spawning habitat is good in the southeast inlet and in the outlet stream.

Although cutthroat trout are native to Sylvan Lake, 2.5 million cutthroat were planted in the lake between 1913 and 1943. In 1978 longnose suckers were found in the lake, probably gaining access from Yellowstone Lake via Clear Creek. Even though Sylvan Lake maintains a good population of cutthroats and has sustained itself as a quality fishery, since 1978 the population of longnose suckers has increased. This situation is causing some concern for longnose suckers can adapt readily to a wide variety of environments and spawning conditions, and these fish may be competing with the cutthroats which require a specific habitat to spawn in—a habitat that is limited to one of the inlets and the outlet. Until 1972, 3 cutthroats per day of any size could be taken from Sylvan Lake. In 1973 the limit dropped to 2 trout per day. In 1978 regulations went to catch-and-release fishing only and this rule remains in effect today.

## 4

# Eleanor Lake

**Location** - On the south side of the East Entrance Highway, 7.6 miles west of the east entrance, 17.5 miles east of Fishing Bridge

**Access** - On the highway

**USGS topographic map** - Eagle Peak, Wyoming

**Size** - 2.4 acres

**Depth** - Maximum 13 feet

**Elevation** - 8450 feet

**Fish type** - Cutthroat trout

Eleanor Lake is a small, narrow and beautiful alpine lake lying alongside the highway just below Sylvan Pass. There is a small picnic area on the west end with room for visitor parking.

The water supply to Eleanor Lake comes from 2 small streams. The inlet stream on the southeast end disappears about 75 feet from the lake and enters through a series of underground seeps. Another small stream enters at the northeast end. There is no outlet stream.

Records indicate that Eleanor Lake was stocked with 28,500 cutthroat trout in 1913. Waters close to Eleanor Lake were regularly stocked with cutthroats in the 1930s and 1940s. It's probable that several additional plants were made into Eleanor Lake during that period.

*Eleanor Lake*

Eleanor Lake's small population of cutthroat trout is somewhat of a mystery. Although it has been stocked and limited spawning habitat does exist, the lake stands a good chance of drying up during low water years because its water supply comes from 2 relatively small streams. Also, because of the lake's shallow depth, the fish are subject to winterkill. In the event of the loss of the fish population, it's unlikely that either of the inlet streams could supply the lake with a viable population of cutthroats. It is possible that during high water years Eleanor Lake develops an outlet flow on the northeast end that connects with Sylvan Lake's outlet about .5 mile northeast of Eleanor Lake. This connection would, for a time, link Eleanor Lake with Sylvan Lake and cutthroat trout could migrate to Eleanor Lake.

# 5

## Riddle Lake

**Location** - Trailhead on the east side of the South Entrance Highway, 2.3 miles south of the junction at Grant Village

**Access** - Foot trail, 2.5 miles

**USGS topographic map** - West Thumb, Wyoming

**Size** - 274 acres

**Depth** - Maximum 27 feet

**Elevation** - 7913 feet

**Fish type** - Cutthroat trout

Riddle Lake, it was once thought, straddled the Continental Divide, with drainages to both the Pacific and Atlantic oceans. Once the actual location of the Continental Divide was determined, the answer to the riddle was found: its only outlet, Solution Creek, flowed into the West Thumb portion of Yellowstone Lake. The Continental Divide is about a mile southwest of Riddle Lake.

The hike to Riddle Lake is through a dense lodgepole pine forest. It is a very easy 30- to 40-minute walk on a flat, well-defined trail. You will cross over the Continental Divide less than .2 mile from the trailhead. This is one trail that you shouldn't hike alone, for this is a high bear-use area and grizzlies are seen often.

Riddle Lake lies in the middle of a dense lodgepole pine forest. There is a marsh that extends from the northwest end of the lake around the west side all the way to the southeast corner. There is another marshy area around the outlet stream on the east side. About the only areas where you can get to the lake on good solid ground are on the north and east sides above Solution Creek and a small area on the east side below the creek. Fortunately, the trail comes out at the north end of the lake, above the marsh.

The major water supply to Riddle Lake comes from snow-melt and seepage. The lake also receives water periodically from several small streams. Its only outlet is Solution Creek.

Because the small streams that feed the lake have water

flowing in them only occasionally, Solution Creek is the only stream used for fish spawning and the conditions there are poor. For several miles downstream from the lake, the current is slow and the bottom consists mainly of muck. There is little gravel in which the trout can build their redds. Solution Creek flows for 8 miles before emptying into Yellowstone Lake. In the lower section of the creek, within 2.5 miles of Yellowstone Lake, cutthroats are able to find conditions suitable for spawning.

Cutthroat trout are native to Riddle Lake, and the first cutthroats to enter the lake came from Yellowstone Lake by migrating up Solution Creek. Today, however, due to the limited spawning conditions of Solution Creek, it is uncertain whether the cutthroats in Riddle Lake originate from spawners in Riddle Lake or Yellowstone Lake.

Because of its close and easy access, Riddle Lake has experienced tremendous fishing pressure. In an attempt to reduce both fishing pressure and kill rates, the Park Service, in June 1974, imposed a limit of 2 fish, each of which had to be less than 14 inches in length. Riddle Lake was used to test the ef-

*Riddle Lake*

fect and overall results of the new regulation in anticipation of the Fish and Wildlife Service's plan to reduce the maximum size limit of Yellowstone Lake's cutthroats to 13 inches. In 1975 Yellowstone Lake went to a 13-inch maximum size limit and Riddle Lake did the same. This still did not reduce the fishing pressure. Riddle Lake's distinction as a quality fishery diminished to the degree that in 1982 it was closed to fishing and it remains closed today.

## OTHER LAKES TO EXPLORE

### 6
### Glade Lake

**Location** - At the base of Mt. Schurz

**Access** - Off-trail travel, 6.8 miles east of the Southeast Arm of Yellowstone Lake

**USGS topographic map** - Eagle Peak, Wyoming

**Size** - 8 acres

**Depth** - Average 9 feet, maximum 15 feet

**Elevation** - 9684 feet

**Fish type** - None

*Chipmunk*

## 7
## Trail
## Lake

**Location** - Approximately 2.5 miles southeast of the Southeast Arm of Yellowstone Lake

**Access** - Heart Lake Trail to Trail Creek Trail, then cross-country following Trail Creek upstream to Trail Lake, approximately 28 miles. By boat from the tip of the Southeast Arm of Yellowstone Lake, you could hike the Trail Creek Trail for about 2 miles before going up Trail Creek to Trail Lake

**USGS topographic map** - Eagle Peak, Wyoming

**Size** - 55 acres

**Depth** - Maximum 12 feet

**Elevation** - 7748 feet

**Fish type** - Cutthroat trout

## 8
## Alder
## Lake

**Location** - Yellowstone Lake Promontory

**Access** - .1 mile east of South Arm

**USGS topographic map** - Frank Island, Wyoming

**Size** - 123 acres

**Depth** - Average 12 feet, maximum 20 feet

**Elevation** - 7752 feet

**Fish type** - Cutthroat trout

## 9
## Mariposa
## Lake

**Location** - Two Ocean Plateau

**Access** - South Boundary Trail, 28 miles

**USGS topographic map** - Two Ocean

Pass, Wyoming
**Size** - 12 acres
**Depth** - Average 4 feet, maximum 7 feet
**Elevation** - 8950 feet
**Fish types** - Cutthroat trout, rainbow–cutthroat hybrids

## 10

# Outlet Lake

**Location** - Approximately 4 miles east of Heart Lake
**Access** - From Heart Lake Trailhead on South Entrance Highway to Trail Creek Trail, 15 miles
**USGS topographic map** - Frank Island, Wyoming
**Size** - 16 acres
**Depth** - Average 3 feet, maximum 5 feet
**Elevation** - 7749 feet
**Fish type** - Cutthroat trout

## 11

# Heart Lake

**Location** - Trailhead located on the east side of the South Entrance Highway, 7.5 miles south of West Thumb and about .5 mile north of Lewis Lake
**Access** - Heart Lake trail, 8 miles
**USGS topographic maps** - West Thumb, Wyoming; Frank Island, Wyoming
**Size** - 2150 acres
**Depth** - Maximum 180 feet
**Elevation** - 7450 feet
**Fish types** - Cutthroat, lake trout

*Lodgepole pines*

## 12
## Sheridan Lake

**Location** - Near Heart Lake
**Access** - Heart Lake Trail, 12 miles
**USGS topographic map** - Huckleberry Mountain, Wyoming
**Size** - 15 acres
**Depth** - Average 1.5 feet, maximum 5 feet
**Elevation** - 7378 feet
**Fish type** - Cutthroat trout

## 13
## Basin Creek Lake

**Location** - Approximately 2.5 miles southwest of Sheridan Lake
**Access** - South Boundary Trail to Heart Lake Trail, 11 miles
**USGS topographic map** - Huckleberry Mountain, Wyoming
**Size** - 8 acres
**Depth** - Maximum 17 feet
**Elevation** - 7390 feet
**Fish type** - Cutthroat trout

## 14
## Forest Lake

**Location** - East of the South Entrance Highway
**Access** - From South Entrance, north on South Entrance Trail, approximately 2.5 miles, then west through dense forest, approximately .3 mile
**USGS topographic map** - Huckleberry Mountain, Wyoming
**Size** - 10 acres

**Depth** - Average 4 feet, maximum 8 feet
**Elevation** - 7421 feet
**Fish type** - None

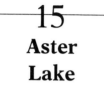

## 15
## Aster Lake

**Location** - Due east of Lewis Lake
**Access** - Off-trail travel, approximately 4 miles up Aster Creek
**USGS topographic map** - West Thumb, Wyoming
**Size** - 14 acres
**Depth** - Unsurveyed, generally deep
**Elevation** - 8141 feet
**Fish type** - None

## 16
## Delusion Lake

**Location** - 1 mile west of Eagle Bay on Yellowstone Lake
**Access** - By boat across Yellowstone Lake, then cross-country for 1 mile, or 4.5 miles cross-country from the West Thumb–South Entrance Highway
**USGS topographic map** - Frank Island, Wyoming
**Size** - 470 acres
**Depth** - Maximum 30 feet
**Elevation** - 7822 feet
**Fish type** - None

*Watching sunset from Shoshone Lake's southeast shore*

# Bechler Region

## OTHER LAKES TO EXPLORE

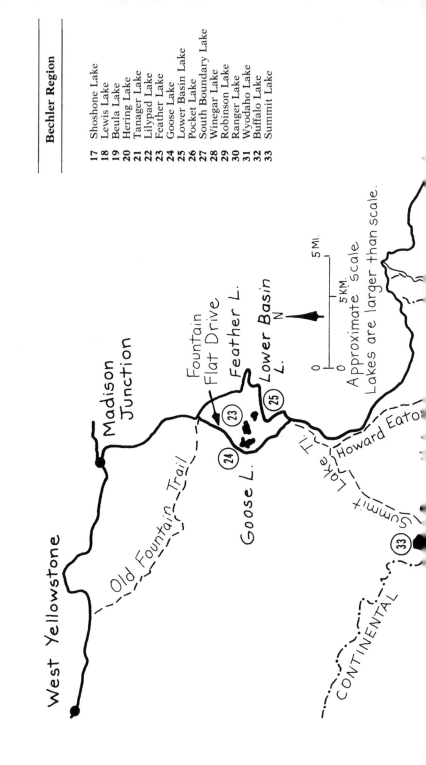

West Yellowstone

Madison Junction

Old Fountain Trail

Fountain Flat Drive

Feather L.

Lower Basin L.

Goose L.

(23)

(24)

(25)

Summit Lake

Howard Eato

(33)

CONTINENTAL

N

5 MI.

5 KM.

Approximate scale
Lakes are larger than scale.

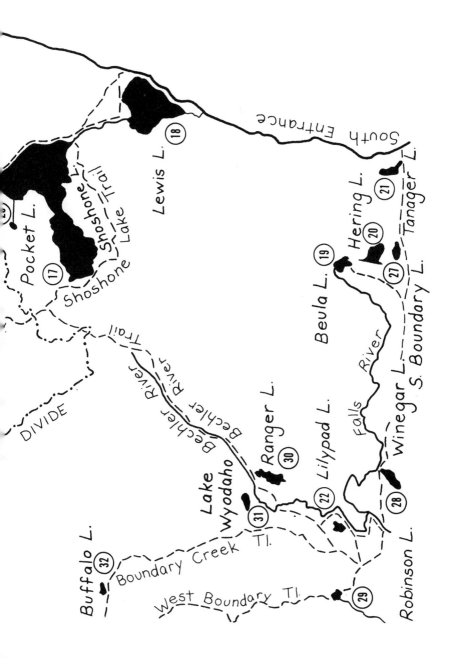

# 17
## Shoshone Lake

**Location** - 3 miles northwest of Lewis Lake

**Access** - Shoshone Lake Trail from Lone Star Trailhead, 9.5 miles; Shoshone Lake Trail from Lewis Trailhead, 4.5 miles; Channel Trail from the Lewis Trailhead, 6 miles; DeLacy Creek Trail, 3 miles; by canoe, approximately 7 miles

**USGS topographic maps** - West Thumb, Wyoming; Old Faithful, Wyoming

**Size** - 8050 acres

**Depth** - Maximum 205 feet

**Elevation** - 7791 feet

**Fish types** - Lake, brown and brook trout

Shoshone Lake is the largest backcountry lake in the lower 48 states and the second largest lake in Yellowstone. Its cold, clear waters range from aquamarine to deep blue where the lake's bottom drops off sharply. (The depth of over 50 percent of the lake exceeds 90 feet.) Shoshone lies in a basin, surrounded by forest and intermittent high bluffs. There are large grassy meadows at the northeastern, southeastern and western ends. These meadows are the sites where the major inlet streams flow into the lake and are good places to see elk and moose. There is always a variety of wildfowl on the lake.

Shoshone Lake can be reached only by foot trail or by hand-propelled boat. Motorized craft are not allowed on the lake. There are 3 trails leading to the lake; the Shoshone Lake Trail, from the Lone Star Trailhead or the Lewis Trailhead, the Channel Trail, also from the Lewis Trailhead, and the DeLacy Creek Trail.

The Lone Star Trailhead is about 2.5 miles east of Old Faithful, near Kepler Cascades on the south side of the highway between Old Faithful and West Thumb. This end of the Shoshone Lake Trail, 9.5 miles to the northwest end of the

*Shoshone Lake*

lake, will take you through the Shoshone Geyser Basin, which contains hot springs and several active geysers.

The Lewis Trailhead is located on the west side of the South Entrance Highway, .7 mile north of Lewis Lake. There are 2 trails from this trailhead, the Shoshone Lake Trail and the Channel Trail. Both trails come out on the southeastern tip of Shoshone Lake. The Channel Trail turns west and parallels the northern shore of Lewis Lake to the Lewis River Channel, which joins Lewis and Shoshone lakes. The trail then turns north, following along the Lewis River to Shoshone Lake, about 6 miles. The Shoshone Lake Trail, on the right, runs in a northwesterly direction through dense forest, 4.5 miles to the lake.

The DeLacy Creek Trail, a 3-mile route to the northeastern tip of the lake, is located 8 miles east of Old Faithful on the south side of the highway.

The 3-mile DeLacy Creek Trail and the 4.5-mile Shoshone Lake Trail, from the Lewis Trailhead, could be used for day hikes, although the overall distance you will travel is, of course, twice that. Once you get to Shoshone Lake, do some exploring or fishing and then hike out, you will have spent most of a day. To travel the 9.5-mile Shoshone Lake Trail from the Lone Star Trailhead, especially with time to explore the Shoshone Geyser Basin, or the 6-mile Channel Trail will require more time and these routes should be reserved for overnight trips.

One of the most exciting ways to get to Shoshone is by canoe. Canoeing provides an opportunity for people who are otherwise not able or are unwilling to hike long distances to experience and enjoy the remoteness of a wilderness. Before you start out, however, make sure you have a boat permit and are thoroughly familiar with the conditions on both Lewis and Shoshone lakes.

The best place to start your trip, is from the Lewis Lake Campground. The boat dock has enough room for you to tie your canoe and lay out your gear. There is also a vehicle parking area just across from the ranger station and your car is safer here than it would be at the parking area on the north end of Lewis Lake. The distance to the lake is a little greater, but the safety factor makes it worth the extra mile or so.

You will, no doubt, see canoes head across the open lake for the Lewis River Channel on the opposite side. This route is faster and shorter, but the decision to cut straight across the lake could quickly lead to a disaster. The southwest winds that blow almost daily on Yellowstone's large lakes spring up suddenly and without warning. Lake conditions can go from dead calm to severe winds and large waves in a very short time. If your canoe were to capsize in the open water, you would probably not make it to shore. Lewis Lake's waters are icy cold, and you could become hypothermic quickly. For your own safety, stay close to the shoreline and go around the lake. That way, if something does happen, your chances of making it ashore without harm are almost assured.

From the Lewis Lake Campground, it's almost 3 miles across to the Lewis River Channel. If you choose to stay close to the shoreline, the distance is 4 miles. Once you reach the channel, it's a 3.5-mile journey upstream to Shoshone Lake. The first 2 miles or so consist of relatively smooth water and are easy to paddle. The last mile is a hand tow because the current is much swifter and there are places so shallow that the bottom of your canoe will drag.

The entire trip will take about 5 hours, depending on your overall physical condition, the weather and the load you are carrying. You should plan to start early and make it to the river channel before the winds on Lewis Lake come up. Once you're in the channel, you will be protected from the winds and can take your time. The passage to Shoshone is a wonderful wilderness experience, with much to see and do. Although the return trip down the Lewis River from Shoshone Lake takes less time, you should still plan to leave early and make your crossing of Lewis Lake before the winds come.

When you get your backcountry permit for overnight camping at Shoshone Lake, you might want to consider picking a campsite that is close to the point where you will come out on the lake. Your energy level won't be what it was when you started out, especially if you have just battled the currents of the Lewis River by canoe. Once you have your camp set up, you can spend the late afternoon and evening simply enjoying the pristine surroundings.

You should plan on a 4- or 5-day minimum stay if you want

*Canoeing on Shoshone Lake*

to explore the entire lake. Shoshone is 6.5 miles long and over 4 miles across at its widest point. That's a lot of shoreline. The campsites along the lake are designated campsites—assigned to specific parties on specific nights. Take this into account when you plan your trip around the lake.

Shoshone Lake was called Snake Lake by early fur trappers, who also used the word "Snake" for the Shoshone Indians. Walter W. DeLacy, the first to map Shoshone Lake, named it DeLacy's Lake in 1863. DeLacy had led a party of prospectors up the Snake River and crossed over into the Madison River area. When Dr. F. V. Hayden, leader of the 1872 Hayden expedition, first saw DeLacy's map, he doubted that DeLacy had ever been to "DeLacy's Lake" because DeLacy's map positioned the lake near the western border of Yellowstone and noted that it drained into the Madison River. DeLacy's 1865 map was indeed inaccurate, but his 1870 map was fairly good and showed that he had, in fact, been to Shoshone Lake. In 1872 F. H. Bradly, chief geologist with the Hayden Expedition, called it Shoshone Lake in honor of the Indian nation.

Shoshone's major water supply is from DeLacy Creek on the northeastern tip, Moose Creek on the southeastern end and Cold Mountain and Shoshone creeks on the western tip. The largest of these inlets is Shoshone Creek. The only outlet is the Lewis River, which flows into Lewis Lake. There is an abundance of spawning habitat in the inlets and the Lewis River outlet.

Historically, Shoshone Lake was barren. In 1890 the lake was stocked with 30,000 lake trout and 3350 brown trout, all yearlings. By 1895 both species were flourishing. The brook trout in Shoshone were stocked in tributary streams and migrated to the lake. Of the 3 species, lake trout rank first in abundance, followed by brown and then brook trout. The largest catch reported was a 34-pound lake trout in August 1975.

# 18
## Lewis Lake

**Location** - On the west side of the South Entrance Highway, 12 miles north of the south entrance

**Access** - On the highway

**USGS topographic map** - West Thumb, Wyoming

**Size** - 2716 acres

**Depth** - Maximum 108 feet

**Elevation** - 7779 feet

**Fish types** - Brown, lake and brook trout

Lewis Lake is the third largest lake in Yellowstone. Its brown and lake trout fishing and easy highway access make its popularity as a lake fishery second only to Yellowstone Lake. The highway parallels Lewis Lake's western shore for 2.5 miles and there are several vehicle turnouts and places to park. The Lewis Lake Campground, located at the south end of the lake, has 100 campsites, boat launching facilities, a ranger station and a vehicle parking area. The Lewis Lake Campground opens the latter part of June, after the ice is gone from the lake, and closes at the end of October. The lake is also the main jumping off point for backcountry travelers who canoe to Shoshone Lake.

Heart-shaped Lewis Lake was named by trappers prior to 1870, in honor of Captain Meriwether Lewis, one of the

*Lewis Lake*

leaders of the Lewis and Clark expedition. The terrain surrounding the lake is mostly forested, except for large meadows on the west, northwest and northeast shores, where the small inlet streams are located. The meadow on the northeast shore around Dogshead Creek is especially wet and marshy. There is an area of hot springs in the meadow on the northwest side and another hot springs area on the west side of the Lewis River outlet at the extreme southern tip of the lake.

The main water supply to Lewis Lake is from Shoshone Lake, 3.5 miles to the northwest. The Lewis River Channel, Shoshone Lake's outlet, connects the two lakes and enters Lewis Lake on the northwest side. There are several other small spring-fed streams that flow into the lake and the area of thermal activity on the northwest shore also contributes to the water supply. The outlet is the Lewis River at the extreme southern tip.

Originally Lewis Lake was barren. The waterfalls in the Lewis River, about half a mile downstream from the lake, prevented upstream migration and there were no fish in Shoshone Lake that could have migrated into Lewis Lake. In 1890 Lewis Lake was stocked with 12,000 lake trout and 3350 Loch Leven brown trout yearlings from Scotland. Both species have done exceptionally well. Sometime before 1940 grayling and cutthroat trout were planted in Lewis Lake, but for some reason these species did not survive. Brook trout have migrated into the lake from several of the inlet streams. Of the 3 species, lake trout rank first in abundance and brook trout are the rarest.

When Lewis Lake was stocked with lake trout in 1890, it was done so with yearlings taken from Lake Michigan. After the Weeland Ship Channel was built to form a passage around Niagara Falls to Lake Erie, opening the Great Lakes to the St. Lawrence River, sea lampreys, an eellike parasite that attaches itself to its prey, bores a hole with its raspy tongue and sucks the blood from its victim, entered the Great Lakes and decimated the population of lake trout in Lake Michigan. Now, with the sea lampreys under control, Fish and Wildlife Service personnel are taking lake trout from Lewis Lake to restock Lake Michigan in the hope that (1) the genetic strain of Lewis Lake trout is still the same pure Lake Michigan strain originally planted and (2) that these restocked lake trout will be able to reproduce in Lake Michigan as the original Lake Michigan trout did in Lewis Lake.

## 19
## Beula Lake

**Location** - Trailhead in the Teton National Forest near Yellowstone's south boundary
**Access** - Foot trail, 2.5 miles
**USGS topographic map** - Grassy Lake Reservoir, Wyoming
**Size** - 107 acres
**Depth** - Maximum 36 feet
**Elevation** - 7377 feet
**Fish type** - Cutthroat trout

The trailhead to Beula Lake is located in the Teton National Forest, on the Ashton-Flagg Road, also called the Reclamation Road, just south of Yellowstone's south boundary. To reach the trailhead, drive 2.1 miles south of Yellowstone's south entrance, then turn west on Ashton-Flagg Road. The road, dirt and gravel and very bumpy at times, isn't too bad if you take your time. It takes about 20 to 30 minutes to travel the 9 miles to the trailhead from the turnoff at the main highway. There is no trailhead marker, but if you look just past the tip of Grassy Lake you will see a small vehicle parking area on the north (right) side of the road and an orange trail marker nailed to a tree. This is the trailhead.

The first few hundred feet of the trail are fairly steep, but the path flattens out on top of the ridge, crosses the South Boundary Trail and remains level until the last 100 yards or so, where you descend to the lake. This is a well-defined, easy-to-follow trail through lodgepole pine. It takes about an hour to walk to the lake.

Beula Lake is a pretty backcountry lake, surrounded by forested hills. Yellow pond lilies and bulrushes are numerous around the outlet on the north end of the lake and the inlets on the south side. The south end around the inlets is also marshy and this is the only place where you will have difficulty getting around the lake. The largest inlet, on the south end, is a wide, shallow, intermittent channel that flows out of nearby Hering Lake. Beula Lake's water supply is furnished by a low gradient stream that enters on the southeast end, intermittent streams and minor spring activity on the north end. Beula Lake is the headwater of the Falls River, which flows from the north side of the lake.

Beula Lake was historically barren because the falls and cascades on the Falls River below the lake prevented fish from migrating up the river and into the lake. Although the origin of fish in the Falls River isn't known, in 1891 trout were recorded in the river as far up as Terraced Falls, about 7 miles below Beula Lake. Between 1935 and 1944, 50,000 cutthroat fry and 1.1 million eyed eggs from the Yellowstone Lake hatchery were planted in Beula Lake and its tributaries. With its good spawning habitat, Beula Lake has been able to maintain a healthy population of cutthroat trout.

*Beula Lake Trail*

*Beula Lake*

# —20— Hering Lake

**Location** - Trailhead in the Teton National Forest near Yellowstone's south boundary

**Access** - Foot trail, 3 miles

**USGS topographic map** - Grassy Lake Reservoir, Wyoming

**Size** - 60 acres

**Depth** - Average 11 feet, maximum 44 feet

**Elevation** - 7381 feet

**Fish type** - Cutthroat trout

The best way to reach Hering Lake is to hike the 2.5 miles to Beula Lake, then follow its shoreline to the southwest end of the lake. Here you will see the small, unmaintained trail that leads to Hering Lake. The trail between the lakes is narrow, but it is flat, easy to follow and only takes about 10 minutes to travel.

You can also hike to Hering Lake by taking the South Boundary Trail to South Boundary Lake, where a similar, unmaintained trail heads north to Hering Lake. This route is considerably longer.

Hering Lake, named in 1878 for Rudolph Hering, a topographer and meterologist with the 1872 Hayden Expedition, is a beautiful backcountry lake surrounded by low hills and a dense lodgepole pine forest. Twelve intermittent streams gather water from an area of about 860 acres and supply water to the lake. Hering's outlet is a wide, shallow creek that flows from the north end of the lake, then empties into Beula Lake.

Although the current size of Hering Lake is 60 acres, an unpublished National Park Service report in 1941 estimated the lake's area at 14.4 acres, and maps published during that time also showed a small lake. Hering Lake's size depends on the amount of annual precipitation in its small drainage. The decade of the 1930s had below normal rainfall and this variation would account for the lake's small size when the 1941 survey was made. The years prior to 1969, when the current

*Unmaintained trail between Beula and Hering lakes,
Hering Lake in background*

lake size was determined, had above normal levels of precipitation.

There are no records that show that historically barren Hering Lake was ever stocked and no one knows when cutthroat trout first entered the lake. It would be reasonable to assume, however, that when nearby Beula Lake and its tributaries were stocked between 1935 and 1944, plants were also made in Hering Lake or the channel that connects the 2 lakes. Another possibility is that the cutthroats migrated from Beula Lake up the channel into Hering Lake during a period of high water. In any event, several of Hering Lake's inlet streams have suitable spawning habitat and the lake has maintained a good population of cutthroat trout.

*Hering Lake*

*Tanager Lake*

## ——21——
## Tanager
## Lake

**Location** - 1 mile west of the Snake River Ranger Station at the south entrance

**Access** - South Boundary Trail, 1 mile

**USGS topographic map** - Huckleberry Mountain, Wyoming

**Size** - 32 acres

**Depth** - Maximum 11 feet

**Elevation** - 6970 feet

**Fish type** - None

Tanager Lake, because of its location and the difficult-to-find South Boundary Trailhead, is seldom visited and has remained in a wild and pristine condition. The trailhead is beside the horse corral, directly behind the Snake River Ranger Station at the south entrance.

The trail climbs rapidly but soon flattens out for a short easy hike through the forest. Although surrounded by lodgepole pine, spruce and subalpine fir, the immediate area around the lake is a wet, boggy meadow. In many places around the shoreline, the ground is so wet that you will start to sink in if you stand in one place long enough. The southern end of Tanager borders Yellowstone's south boundary and because of its marshy environment and undisturbed setting, it is a good place to see and photograph moose and a variety of waterfowl and bird life.

Tanager Lake's water supply originates from several seeps on the lake's north end and from a spring on the east side. The outlet is at the tip of the southwest end. Records do not indicate that Tanager Lake has been stocked with sport fish, although the lake does contain a healthy population of redside shiners, minnows that are native to this part of the Snake River drainage.

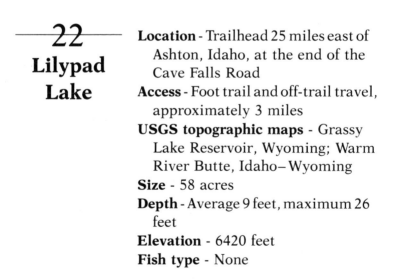

## 22
## Lilypad Lake

**Location** - Trailhead 25 miles east of Ashton, Idaho, at the end of the Cave Falls Road

**Access** - Foot trail and off-trail travel, approximately 3 miles

**USGS topographic maps** - Grassy Lake Reservoir, Wyoming; Warm River Butte, Idaho–Wyoming

**Size** - 58 acres

**Depth** - Average 9 feet, maximum 26 feet

**Elevation** - 6420 feet

**Fish type** - None

Lilypad Lake lies in the remote southwestern corner of Yellowstone, an area of the park that most visitors never see. This part of the Falls River Basin is relatively flat, with heavy forest, and is highlighted by 2 beautiful rivers, the Falls and the Bechler.

*Loon on Lilypad Lake*

To reach this part of Yellowstone and the trail to Lilypad Lake, you must drive to Ashton, Idaho, about half way between West Yellowstone and Idaho Falls. From Ashton, travel east on Idaho 47 and the Cave Falls Road 25 miles to the end of the road and the trailhead.

The trail to Lilypad Lake is the Bechler River Trail, which begins at Cave Falls. The trail follows the west side of the Falls River for about .3 mile, to the point where the Bechler River flows into the Falls. Here the Falls River turns east and the trail continues along the Bechler. The hike is easy and enjoyable. The country is beautiful and the fishing for cutthroat and rainbow trout is good along the river.

You will need a compass and the Warm River Butte, Idaho – Wyoming, 15-minute topographic map to know where to leave the trail to reach Lilypad Lake. If you leave the trail at the right location, the southwestern end of the lake will be .2 mile from the trail. Follow the topographic map closely and use your compass. If you are not sure of the map or your ability to find the lake, don't attempt to go to Lilypad. Getting lost in this area of Yellowstone would be a bad experience.

Once you leave the trail, the hike to the lake is through heavy lodgepole pine. The undergrowth is not excessively dense and walking is fairly easy except in areas where you will have to pick your way around or over downfalls.

Lilypad Lake lives up to its name: more than half the lake is covered with yellow pond lilies. The shoreline of the lake is grassy, although some areas may be a little wet and boggy, and you can get around Lilypad without much problem. Lodgepole pines surround the basin and huckleberry bushes around the lake are numerous.

You will more than likely have Lilypad Lake all to yourself. It's a good place to see and photograph loons, trumpeter swans, sandhill cranes and a variety of ducks. Elk and moose can be seen around the large meadow to the southwest. Lilypad Lake was stocked with 4400 cutthroat trout in 1937, but due to the lack of spawning habitat, the cutthroat were not able to sustain themselves, and the lake is barren.

The main water supply for Lilypad Lake is the seepage along the western side. There is also a small inlet on the west side but its water flow is minimal. The main outlet is at the southeastern end of the lake; its flow is also minimal.

## 23

# Feather
# Lake

**Location** - At the end of Fountain
Flat Drive, 3.4 miles from the
turnoff of the Old Faithful–
Madison Junction Highway
**Access** - Gravel road
**USGS topographic map** - Madison
Junction, Wyoming
**Size** - 17.5 acres
**Depth** - Maximum 30 feet
**Elevation** - 7170 feet
**Fish type** - None

To get to Feather Lake, you must take the Fountain Flat
Drive, which is located on the west side of the Old Faithful–
Madison Junction Highway, 10.5 miles north of Old Faithful
and 5.5 miles south of Madison Junction. This is a pretty
drive that begins across an open meadow, following along the
Firehole River. At 1.6 miles there is a warning sign indicating
a rough road ahead and suggesting that you should turn
around here. At 1.8 miles the pavement ends and a well-
maintained gravel road begins. At 2.5 miles you will pass
Goose Lake on the left and the turn to the Goose Lake picnic
area. At 3 miles drivers must make a left-hand turn toward
Feather Lake. The road continues on to the right, to Fairy
Falls, 2.2 miles, and Imperial Geyser, 2.8 miles, but is closed
to motor vehicles. The road, a little bumpy and narrow, follows the Firehole River, which flows through a grassy
meadow. At 3.4 miles, the road ends at the Feather Lake picnic area and Feather Lake.

There are picnic tables and restrooms at Feather Lake and
ample room for vehicle parking. Camping is prohibited, however, and campfires are not allowed.

Feather Lake lies in a natural depression formed by volcanic and geyser activity. It lies about 40 feet below the
plateau and is surrounded by lodgepole pines. The bank
around the lake is fairly steep and the ground along the
shoreline is solid. Hiking around the lake is easy.

Underground springs and seepage feed Feather Lake; there

*Above: Feather Lake picnic area.*
*Below: Firehole River near Feather Lake*

is no inlet or outlet stream. Because of its lack of spawning habitat, Feather Lake has no fish, even though it was unofficially stocked with yellow perch sometime before 1919. The perch disappeared after a few years because the lake lacked the aquatic vegetation that the yellow perch needed to spawn successfully.

Stocking records also show that 3060 rainbow trout were planted in Feather Lake in 1936, 1000 in 1954 and another 1000 in 1956. The rainbow have also disappeared due to the lack of spawning habitat.

The nice thing about Feather Lake is that you can drive to it and still enjoy a certain degree of seclusion. There are usually few people this far back on Fountain Flat Drive. Most visitors turn around at the point where Fountain Flat Drive becomes a gravel road. The Feather Lake area is a beautiful part of the park and, if you're lucky, you might have it all to yourself.

About .1 mile northwest of Feather Lake, near the northeast corner of Goose Lake, is a small, fishless, 3-acre lake with a maximum depth around 5 feet. There is no trail leading from Feather Lake to this tiny lake, but the walk is an easy one. You should have the Madison Junction, Wyoming, topographic map and a compass to be sure you are headed in the right direction.

This Gosling, as it has been called, is a small, circular lake ringed with bulrushes. There is a meadow, which is quite pretty and enjoyable to walk around on the north end of the lake. There is a variety of wildflowers and bird life, and your chances of seeing deer and elk in the morning and evening are good.

## 24
# Goose Lake

**Location** - On Fountain Flat Drive, 2.5 miles from the turnoff of the Old Faithful–Madison Junction Highway

**Access** - Gravel road

**USGS topographic map** - Madison Junction, Wyoming

**Size** - 34 acres

*Goose Lake*

**Depth** - Maximum 31 feet
**Elevation** - 7170 feet
**Fish type** - Rainbow trout

To get to Goose Lake, take the Fountain Flat Drive turnoff on the west side of the Old Faithful–Madison Junction Highway, 10.5 miles north of Old Faithful and 5.5 miles south of Madison Junction. At 2.5 miles you will see Goose Lake on the left and the turn to the Goose Lake picnic area. The picnic area sits among the trees, right on the lake, and has tables, restrooms and plenty of room for vehicle parking. Camping is not allowed in the picnic area and you cannot build a camp-fire. The main road follows along the southwest side of Goose Lake for .4 mile. There are other places where you can drive down to the lake and find more privacy than the picnic area has to offer.

Like the other lakes in this area, Goose Lake lies in a natural depression formed by geyser and volcanic activity. Lodgepole pines surround the lake, and although the southwest corner and south end are marshy, most of the ground around the lake is solid.

There is no outlet stream from Goose Lake, but there is a small inlet located at the southwestern end. The volume of water that enters the lake is low, however. There are standing dead trees in the lake, close to the shoreline, which indicates that the water level has risen in recent years. This increase may be attributed to higher-than-average spring runoff or an additional water source, such as an underground spring.

Although no official stocking records exist of this historically barren lake, yellow perch were found in Goose Lake in 1919. Records do show that nearby Feather Lake was unofficially stocked with yellow perch prior to 1919 and it seems reasonable to assume that Goose Lake was stocked with the same species at the same time. Goose Lake was officially stocked with brown trout in 1933. One record reports the number at 108,800, while another shows that 13,400 trout were released. Large trout were reported in the lake in 1936, but research conducted that fall indicated that the browns were not spawning and they eventually disappeared. In 1937 the National Park Service recommended that the yellow perch be chemically removed from the lake and the recommendation was carried out in 1938. Goose Lake was restocked with 48,400 rainbow trout in 1939 and another 2000 in 1956. During a survey in 1966, 3 brook trout were found in Goose Lake. Since the inlet stream is barren and, even during periods of high water, there is no link with nearby Firehole River, the trout must have been transplanted, perhaps by fishermen.

Although Goose Lake has been a productive fishery in past years and was supported by restocking, fishing today is poor. With the low volume of inflow water and no outlet, rainbow trout spawning is limited and may not take place at all during the low-water years. Goose Lake will probably never be able to maintain more than a marginal population of wild trout.

## 25
## Lower Basin Lake

**Location** - 100 yards west of the Madison Junction–Old Faithful Highway, .1 mile south of Firehole Lake Drive

**Access** - Near the highway, unmaintained trail

**USGS topographic map** - Madison Junction, Wyoming

**Size** - Approximately 5 acres

**Depth** - Unsurveyed

**Elevation** - 7240 feet

**Fish type** - None

Just south of the entrance to Firehole Lake Drive, there is a small, gravel turnout on the west side of the highway. From the turnout, facing the trees, you will see a small hill in front

*Firehole Lake's Steady Geyser*

of you to the right. To the left of the hill, where it slopes downward, there is a small clearing and a narrow, unmaintained trail—more like a footpath or a game trail—that will take you to Lower Basin Lake.

The lake basin is a small depression, surrounded by trees, about 100 yards from the turnout. There are a variety of ducks and Canada geese on the lake and wildflowers cover the narrow meadows on the south and west ends of the lake. Although close to the highway, Lower Basin Lake is a secluded and peaceful area to visit.

# OTHER LAKES TO EXPLORE

## 26
## Pocket Lake

**Location** - 1.1 miles west of the northwest end of Shoshone Lake

**Access** - Off-trail travel

**USGS topographic map** - West Thumb, Wyoming

**Size** - 14 acres

**Depth** - Maximum 24 feet

**Elevation** - 8100 feet

**Fish type** - Cutthroat trout

## 27
## South Boundary Lake

**Location** - 2 miles west of the south entrance

**Access** - South Boundary Trail, 2 miles

**USGS topographic map** - Grassy Lake Reservoir, Wyoming

**Size** - 10 acres

**Depth** - Unsurveyed, shallow

**Elevation** - 7400 feet

**Fish type** - None

*Bear warning signs are commonly seen throughout Yellowstone's backcountry*

## 28
## Winegar Lake

**Location** - East of Cave Falls on Yellowstone's south boundary

**Access** - South Boundary Trail, 4 miles

**USGS topographic map** - Grassy Lake Reservoir, Wyoming

**Size** - 28.5 acres

**Depth** - Average 12 feet, maximum 26 feet

**Elevation** - 6460 feet

**Fish type** - None

## 29
# Robinson Lake

**Location** - 2 miles northwest of the Bechler Ranger Station
**Access** - West Boundary Trail from Bechler Ranger Station, 2 miles
**USGS topographic map** - Warm River Butte, Idaho–Wyoming
**Size** - 35 acres
**Depth** - Average 4 feet, maximum 8 feet
**Elevation** - 6500 feet
**Fish type** - None

## 30
# Ranger Lake

**Location** - Northeast of Bechler Meadows
**Access** - Bechler River Trail from Cave Falls, approximately 8 miles, then cross-country for .25 to .5 miles, depending on the point at which you leave the trail
**USGS topographic map** - Grassy Lake Reservoir, Wyoming
**Size** - 58 acres
**Depth** - Average 38 feet, maximum 98 feet
**Elevation** - 6980 feet
**Fish type** - Rainbow trout

## 31
# Wyodaho Lake

**Location** - At the southern edge of the Madison Plateau
**Access** - Bechler River Trail, approximately 7 miles; or the Bechler Meadows Trail to the Bechler

River Trail, 8 miles, then cross-country, about 1 mile
**USGS topographic map** - Grassy Lake Reservoir, Wyoming
**Size** - 12 acres
**Depth** - Average 14 feet, maximum 33 feet
**Elevation** - 6796 feet
**Fish type** - None

## 32
## Buffalo Lake

**Location** - On the Madison Plateau
**Access** - Boundary Creek Trail, 16 miles
**USGS topographic map** - Buffalo Lake, Montana
**Size** - 20 acres
**Depth** - Average 6 feet, maximum 16 feet
**Elevation** - 7700 feet
**Fish type** - None

## 33
## Summit Lake

**Location** - On the Madison Plateau near the Continental Divide
**Access** - Summit Lake Trail, 7.5 miles
**USGS topographic map** - Old Faithful, Wyoming
**Size** - 28.5 acres
**Depth** - Average 8 feet, maximum 21 feet
**Elevation** - 8552 feet
**Fish type** - None

# Central Plateau Region

*Left: Isa Lake*

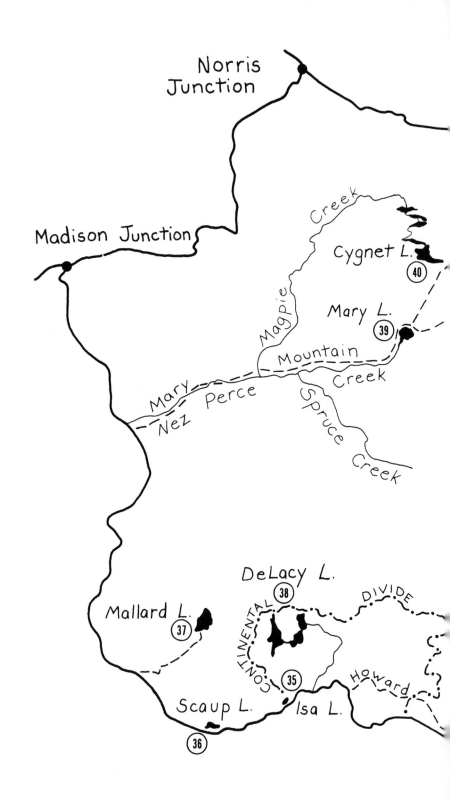

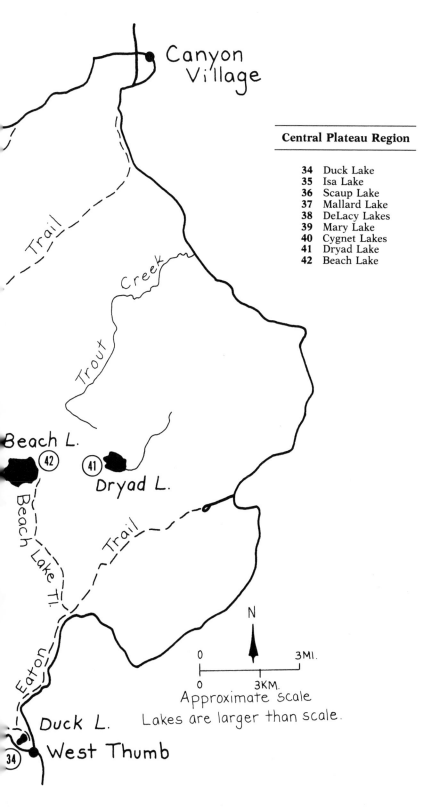

Canyon Village

**Central Plateau Region**

| | |
|---|---|
| **34** | Duck Lake |
| **35** | Isa Lake |
| **36** | Scaup Lake |
| **37** | Mallard Lake |
| **38** | DeLacy Lakes |
| **39** | Mary Lake |
| **40** | Cygnet Lakes |
| **41** | Dryad Lake |
| **42** | Beach Lake |

Trail

Trout Creek

Beach L.
(42)

(41) Dryad L.

Beach Lake Tl.

Trail

Eaton

N

0         3 MI.

0     3 KM.
Approximate scale
Lakes are larger than scale.

Duck L.
(34) West Thumb

# 34

## Duck Lake

**Location** - On the north side of the West Thumb–Old Faithful Highway, .3 mile west of West Thumb

**Access** - Near the highway

**USGS topographic map** - West Thumb, Wyoming

**Size** - 37 acres

**Depth** - Maximum 60 feet

**Elevation** - 7770 feet

**Fish type** - None

Duck Lake lies in a deep basin completely surrounded by a dense forest of lodgepole pine, spruce and fir. Because of the trees and the location of the lake, about 250 feet below the highway, you have to be looking for it or you'll miss it completely. There is an old service road .3 mile from West Thumb that leads down to the lake but, since the service road is closed to vehicle traffic you have to park at a turnout another .1 mile past the lake, walk back to the service road and down to the lake. The road is somewhat steep but it's an easy walking distance.

Duck Lake is a pretty lake, private and secluded. Unfortunately, the West Thumb domestic water-pumping station is located on the southwest shore of the lake and detracts from the beauty of the area.

Two small inlets on the west side provide Duck Lake's water supply. There is no outlet.

Originally barren, Duck Lake received its first stocking of 290,000 cutthroat trout in 1903. It was again stocked with cutthroat in 1905, 1906 and 1912. Landlocked salmon were introduced in 1908 and brown trout in 1938. A total of 655,000 cutthroats, 2000 landlocked salmon and 31,600 brown trout were planted in Duck Lake. By 1965 brown trout was the only species that remained and because the lake's water was used for domestic purposes at West Thumb, it was closed to fishing.

In 1965 the Park Service initiated a survey, which recommended that Duck Lake be chemically treated for the re-

*Duck Lake*

moval of the remaining brown trout. The trout that were studied during the survey showed poor body condition and although they had been able to sustain themselves somewhat by spawning in 2 small tributaries, their spawning did not occur each year. Also, because Duck Lake was only .2 mile from Yellowstone Lake the possibility existed of an accidental introduction of brown trout into Yellowstone Lake during a period of extreme high water. On September 23, 1967 the remaining brown trout were chemically removed from Duck Lake.

## 35
## Isa
## Lake

**Location** - On the north side of the West Thumb–Old Faithful Highway, 9.7 miles west of West Thumb

**Access** - On the highway

**USGS topographic map** - West Thumb, Wyoming

**Size** - Approximately 1 acre

**Depth** - Unsurveyed, generally shallow

**Elevation** - 8262 feet

**Fish type** - None

Tiny Isa Lake, covered with yellow pond lilies in midsummer, is an unusual and very popular lake. There is a large turnout on the north side of the highway to accommodate the cars and buses that stop. Isa straddles the Continental Divide and its drainages flow into the Pacific Ocean and the Gulf of Mexico. During spring runoff, Isa Lake's eastern outlet flows into DeLacy Creek, through Shoshone Lake, into the Lewis, Snake and Columbia rivers to the Pacific Ocean. Its western outlet drains into Spring Creek, the Firehole, Madison, Missouri and Mississippi rivers to the Gulf of Mexico. Isa Lake was named by the Northern Pacific Railroad in 1895 for Isabelle Jelke, the first official tourist to visit the lake.

## 36
## Scaup
## Lake

**Location** - On the north side of the Old Faithful–West Thumb Highway, 4.5 miles east of Old Faithful

**Access** - On the highway

**USGS topographic map** - Old Faithful, Wyoming

**Size** - 5 acres

**Depth** - Maximum 10 feet

**Elevation** - 7900 feet

**Fish type** - None

*Isa Lake*

*Scaup Lake*

Scaup Lake is a pretty little lake that is set in a small glacial basin surrounded by lodgepole pine. The large vehicle turn-out on the highway, right at the lake, is probably the reason why so many people fish in this fishless lake. Because of its shallow depth and the absence of an inlet and outlet stream, there are no fish in the lake and records indicate that it has never been stocked. Underground seepage could contribute to Scaup's water supply, but the likeliest source is runoff from melting snow.

## 37
## Mallard Lake

**Location** - Near Old Faithful
**Access** - Foot trail, 3.3 miles
**USGS topographic map** - Old Faithful, Wyoming
**Size** - 32 acres
**Depth** - Maximum 30 feet
**Elevation** - 8026 feet
**Fish type** - None

The trailhead to Mallard Lake begins at the back of the cabin area behind Old Faithful Lodge. There is a footbridge where

*Mallard Lake*

*Yellow-headed blackbird*

the trail crosses the Firehole River and enters a lodgepole pine forest. This a pleasant, easy hike, with a slight climb on a trail wide enough in places to be a road. You will see a thermal area to your left soon after you start. A mud pot, several small hot pools and tiny, delicate thermal features are scattered about and make this an interesting area to explore. The trail continues through heavy forest and you will not see Mallard Lake until you are almost there.

The lake basin is completely surrounded by lodgepole pine. Trees hug most of the shoreline, but getting around the lake is not difficult. There are a variety of ducks on the lake and interesting bird life can be viewed around the lake. There is even the possibility of seeing a rare great gray owl. The lake has several campsites and a restroom. These conveniences do detract from the beauty and serene environment of Mallard Lake, but the lake's location near Old Faithful makes it a popular destination and it is visited often.

Originally barren, Mallard Lake was heavily stocked with cutthroat trout. For 9 years, between 1934 and 1943, 120,200 eggs and 197,700 cutthroat fry and fingerlings from Yellowstone Lake were planted in Mallard Lake. It is not a good fishery, however, because of poor spawning habitat. Its water supply comes from snowmelt and seepage and there is no inlet stream. There is an outlet that could provide spawning habitat, but the stream flows only during high-water periods in the spring and is dry the rest of the year. As late as 1970 Mallard Lake held a few cutthroat; today, it appears barren.

# OTHER LAKES TO EXPLORE

## 38
## DeLacy
## Lakes

**Location** - North of the Old Faithful–West Thumb Highway

**Access** - Off-trail travel, approximately 3.5 miles up DeLacy Creek from the point where DeLacy crosses the highway about 1 mile east of Isa Lake.

**USGS topographic map** - West Thumb, Wyoming

**Sizes** - 3 lakes, combined area of 60 acres

**Depths** - Maximums west lake 50 feet, middle lake 25 feet, east lake 42 feet

**Elevation** - 8516 feet

**Fish type** - None

## 39
## Mary Lake

**Location** - Near Mary Mountain

**Access** - Mary Mountain Trail, 11 miles from trailhead on Madison Junction–Old Faithful Highway; 9 miles from trailhead on Canyon Village–Lake Highway

**USGS topographic map** - Norris Junction, Wyoming

**Size** - 20 acres

**Depth** - Average 17 feet, maximum 35 feet

**Elevation** - 8266 feet

**Fish type** - None

## 40
## Cygnet Lakes

**Location** - South of the Canyon–Norris Highway

**Access** - Unmaintained trail, approximately 4 miles; trailhead on the south side of the Canyon–Norris Highway, 4.5 miles west of Canyon Village

**USGS topographic map** - Norris Junction, Wyoming

**Sizes** - 5 lakes vary from 6 to 19 acres

**Depths** - 5 lakes vary from 11 to 17 feet

**Elevation** - 8300 feet

**Fish type** - None

## 41
## Dryad Lake

**Location** - Near Elephant Bank Mountain

**Access** - Off-trail travel, approximately 4 miles west of Yellowstone Lake's Bridge Bay

**USGS topographic map** - Norris
   Junction, Wyoming
**Size** - 44 acres
**Depth** - Average 8 feet, maximum 25
   feet
**Elevation** - 8298 feet
**Fish type** - None

## 42
## Beach
## Lake

**Location** - Near Arnica Creek
**Access** - Beach Lake Trail, 5.5 miles
**USGS topographic map** - Norris
   Junction, Wyoming
**Size** - 84 acres
**Depth** - Maximum 30 feet
**Elevation** - 8146 feet
**Fish type** - None

*Harebells*

*Antelope*

# Gallatin Region

**OTHER LAKES TO EXPLORE**

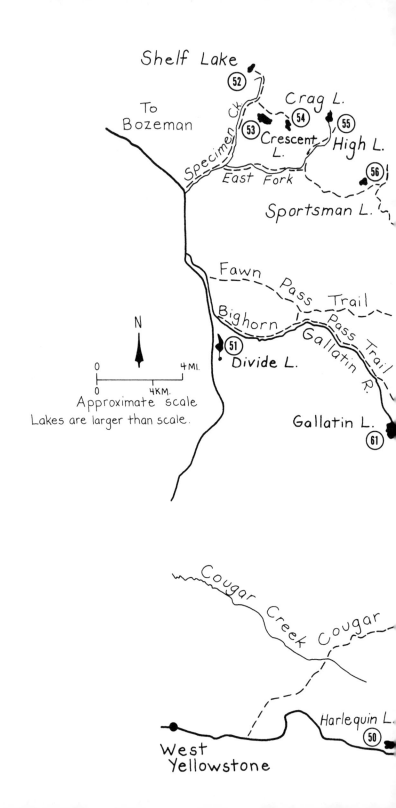

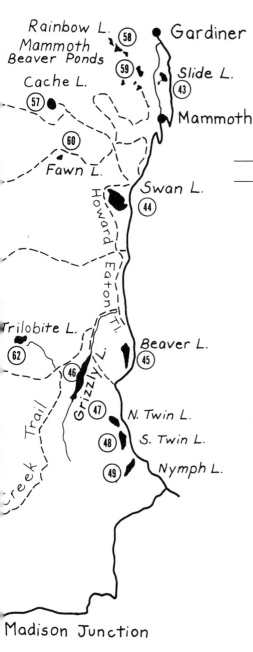

## Gallatin Region

| | |
|---|---|
| 43 | Slide Lakes |
| 44 | Swan Lake |
| 45 | Beaver Lake |
| 46 | Grizzly Lake |
| 47 | North Twin Lake |
| 48 | South Twin Lake |
| 49 | Nymph Lake |
| 50 | Harlequin Lake |
| 51 | Divide Lake |
| 52 | Shelf Lake |
| 53 | Crescent Lake |
| 54 | Crag Lake |
| 55 | High Lake |
| 56 | Sportsman Lake |
| 57 | Cache Lake |
| 58 | Rainbow Lakes |
| 59 | Mammoth Beaver Ponds |
| 60 | Fawn Lake |
| 61 | Gallatin Lake |
| 62 | Trilobite Lake |

# 43

## Slide Lakes

**Location** - Below the east side of the Old Gardiner Road, 1.9 miles north of Mammoth Hot Springs

**Access** - Dirt road, off-trail travel, .2 mile

**USGS topographic map** - Gardiner, Montana

**Sizes** - Big Slide Lake 4 acres, Little Slide Lake 1 acre

**Depths** - Big Slide Lake maximum 17 feet, Little Slide Lake maximum 9 feet

**Elevations** - Big Slide Lake 5670 feet, Little Slide Lake 5710 feet

**Fish type** - Big Slide Lake, none; Little Slide Lake, rainbow trout

The Old Gardiner Road is a narrow, one-way dirt road open to travel only during daylight hours. It begins behind Mammoth Hot Springs Hotel and comes out, 3.9 miles farther, at the North Entrance Station. This enjoyable side trip offers good views of the Gardiner Canyon and its rocky, sage-covered hillsides. Big Slide Lake will come into view on the right side, below the road, at 1.7 miles. At 1.9 miles you will come upon a narrow line of trees and see a small vehicle turnout, where you can park. At this point, Big Slide Lake is directly below you, and you can hike down to the lake, about .2 mile, by following the trees.

Big Slide and Little Slide were formed by mudflows that dammed the small inlet stream. The inlet flows from the fishless Beaver Ponds about .5 mile southwest, at the base of 9652-foot Sepulcher Mountain, enters the small lake at the western tip, flows out of the north end of the lake and enters the large lake about 200 feet northeast. The stream exits Big Slide Lake on the north end, then drops down the steep canyon into the Gardiner River.

The opportunities to see and photograph wildlife are good, because the Old Gardiner Road is not well traveled and the

*Slide Lake*

lakes are seldom visited. Antelope can be seen close to the road almost anytime of the day; deer, elk and coyote can be seen on the hillsides and around the lake early in the morning and late in the evening. Yellow-headed and red-winged blackbirds are plentiful in the sedge grass that surrounds the shoreline of both lakes and there is almost always a variety of ducks on the lakes. Bears are seen quite often in this part of Yellowstone and it's worthwhile to check at the Mammoth Ranger Station to ascertain the current bear situation. Hiking is often restricted in this area.

There is a small population of rainbow trout in Little Slide Lake and curiously, no fish whatsoever in Big Slide Lake. Records indicate that both lakes were historically barren and that during a 12-year period, from 1936 through 1952, 66,800 rainbow trout were planted in Big Slide Lake. Such frequent stocking would suggest either high catch rates that depleted the fish population or, more likely, winterkill that occurred frequently. Of course, it is possible that rainbow trout were stocked in both lakes and were able to sustain themselves only in the small lake. Spawning habitat is poor in both lakes but the rocky inlet of Little Slide Lake could be used by spawning trout. If the small lake wasn't stocked, the fish could have migrated from Big Slide Lake—there are no impassable barriers in the short stream that connects the two lakes. It could be that the inlet stream flows through Little Slide Lake at such a rate that it prevents winterkill by providing enough oxygen to the shallow water that it doesn't freeze solid in the winter. No one really knows.

## 44

### Swan Lake

**Location** - On the west side of the Mammoth–Norris Highway, 5 miles south of Mammoth Hot Springs

**Access** - Near the highway

**USGS topographic map** - Mammoth, Wyoming–Montana

**Size** - 40 acres

**Depth** - Maximum 3 feet

**Elevation** - 7267 feet

**Fish type** - None

Swan Lake lies in a large grass- and sage-covered meadow called Swan Lake Flat, on the eastern edge of Gardner's Hole. The large turnout on the highway is a popular stopping point for visitors because of the geology exhibit about 9944-foot Quadrant Mountain and because the marshy environment surrounding the lake attracts waterfowl and bird life.

The presence of swans on the lake led Colonel P. W. Norris to name it Swan Lake in 1879. Norris was the leader of the 1875 Norris Expedition ·to Yellowstone and in 1877 became the second superintendent of the park.

The lake is about 500 feet from the vehicle turnout and the two are connected by a trail that is usually dry in the otherwise marshy environment around the lake.

Brook trout were planted in Swan Lake in 1905 and 1908, but they didn't survive the lake's shallow depth and the insuf-

*Gardiner River below Slide Lakes at 45th parallel,*
*halfway between the North and South Poles*

ficient flow of the inlet and outlet streams. Swan Lake's water supply comes from a spring-fed inlet that enters the lake at the northwest tip. The outlet stream flows from the east side of the lake and into a rock culvert under the highway. The rate of flow in both the inlet and the outlet is almost unnoticeable, however, and without sufficient intensity to carry away the fine-grained alluvial deposits settling in the lake basin, Swan Lake will dwindle in size and eventually become a grassy marsh.

*Beaver Lake*

## 45

## Beaver Lake

**Location** - On the west side of the Norris–Mammoth Highway, 7.6 miles north of Norris Junction

**Access** - On the highway

**USGS topographic map** - Mammoth, Wyoming–Montana

**Size** - 22 acres

**Depth** - Average 1.2 feet, maximum 4 feet

**Elevation** - 7380 feet

**Fish type** - Brook trout

Beaver Lake is not easy to reach, even though it's located right beside the highway. You can see the entire lake as you drive by, but there is no vehicle turnout or parking area at the lake.

If you decide to stop at the small turnout about 200 feet south of the lake or at the Beaver Lake picnic area, about 500 feet south, and walk to the lake, you will find that Beaver

Lake is difficult to get around. The south end is a mud flat and you can't get close to the lake without getting wet and muddy. The west and north ends are marshy and the eastern edge has a steep incline that makes walking difficult.

The water in Beaver Lake looks brown and muddy. In fact it is extremely clear. Its appearance is due to its shallow depth and brown, silty bottom. A small stream enters from the south end and there are several seeps that flow from the marshy area west of the lake. Obsidian Creek enters Beaver Lake through several channels from a small pond on the west side, then exits from the north end. In time the rapid accumulation of silt will cause the disappearance of Beaver Lake and Obsidian Creek will flow freely through a grassy marshland.

Beaver Lake was never officially stocked with brook trout, but Obsidian Creek was stocked several times between 1901 and 1952 and this seems the likely source for the lake's population of small brookies. Beaver Lake was stocked with rainbow trout in 1895 and grayling in 1935 and 1937, but they have since disappeared.

Beaver Lake was formed by a beaver dam. You can still see the remains of a beaver lodge in the northwestern part of the lake. The beaver disappeared from the lake years ago.

## 46
## Grizzly Lake

**Location** - Trailhead on the west side of the Mammoth–Norris Highway, 6.2 miles north of Norris Junction

**Access** - Foot trail, 1.8 miles

**USGS topographic map** - Mt. Holmes, Wyoming–Montana

**Size** - 136 acres

**Depth** - Maximum 36 feet

**Elevation** - 7508 feet

**Fish type** - Brook trout

About 1.5 miles south of Beaver Lake, there is a small vehicle turnout and a trailhead sign on the west side of the highway.

The hike to Grizzly Lake takes about 45 to 60 minutes, depending on your physical condition. It's one of those hikes that the Rocky Mountains are famous for: uphill both ways. After crossing an open, grassy meadow that can be quite wet and marshy in the spring and early summer, the steep trail makes a series of switchbacks that will take you to the top of a narrow ridge. From this point the trail descends about .3 mile through the forest to the north end of Grizzly Lake. The peak you can see in the background is the 10,336-foot Mt. Holmes.

Grizzly Lake is an absolutely gorgeous lake, long and narrow, nestled between 2 high ridges. Except for the meadow on the south end, the lake is bordered by a dense forest of lodgepole pine, spruce and fir. The ground is solid and walking around the lake is not difficult, except at the north and south ends, where it can be marshy.

There is a peace and calm at Grizzly Lake that is hard sometimes, to imagine. It's so quiet that all you can hear is

*Grizzly Lake*

the breeze in the forest and the cold, clear water lapping against the shore. The air has a sweet, piney smell that is clean and fresh. Even when there are other people at the lake, and this popular lake sees both day hikers and backcountry campers, Grizzly is big enough and long enough that you can feel that you have it all to yourself.

Grizzly Lake's water supply comes from Straight Creek at the southwest end. There are additional small streams and seeps that enter the lake, mainly from the west side. Straight Creek is also the outlet stream, and the creek provides good spawning habitat in both the inlet and the outlet. Good spawning habitat also exists in several of the other inlet streams.

Grizzly Lake was originally barren and there are no records to indicate that it was ever stocked. Obsidian Creek was stocked with brook trout between 1901 and 1952 and Winter Creek was stocked with 8000 brook trout in 1928. Grizzly Lake's outlet, Straight Creek, connects with both streams and is the probable source of the lake's pan-size brook trout.

## 47
## North Twin Lake

**Location** - On the west side of the Mammoth–Norris Highway, 3.7 miles north of Norris Junction

**Access** - Near the highway

**USGS topographic map** - Mammoth, Wyoming–Montana

**Size** - 10 acres

**Depth** - Maximum 11 feet

**Elevation** - 7550 feet

**Fish type** - None

North Twin Lake lies in a small basin formed by volcanic and geyser activity. The lake, which is near the highway, is surrounded by forest, with pretty sedge grass meadows bordering the shore on the north and south ends. Historically fishless, records show that 1000 mountain whitefish were

*North Twin Lake*

planted in 1889. By 1899 North Twin had returned to a barren state. In 1934 and 1935, 135,000 grayling were stocked but they also disappeared. Because of its shallow depth and lack of an inlet and outlet stream (its water supply comes from spring and geyser activity), North Twin Lake is not a suitable fishery.

## ──48── South Twin Lake

**Location** - On the west side of the Mammoth–Norris Highway, 3.3 miles north of Norris Junction

**Access** - Near the highway

**USGS topographic map** - Mammoth, Wyoming–Montana

**Size** - 14 acres

**Depth** - Maximum 29 feet

**Elevation** - 7529 feet

**Fish type** - None

Although barren today, South Twin Lake, for a time, seemed able to support a fish population. It was stocked with 1000 mountain whitefish in 1889 and 200 rainbow trout in 1933. From 1934 to 1956, over 450,000 grayling were planted in the lake. As late as 1964 grayling were still being taken from South Twin Lake. Although no records exist to show that cutthroat trout were ever stocked, they were also taken from the lake in 1964.

Unlike its northern twin, South Twin Lake has suitable water temperature and depth and enough food to ensure a fish population's growth and survival. Like its twin, however, the water supply comes from springs and geyser activity. With no inlet and no outlet stream, the lack of spawning habitat caused South Twin Lake to return to its barren condition.

*South Twin Lake*

*A bubbling hot spring draining into Nymph Lake*

# 49
# Nymph Lake

**Location** - On the west side of the Norris Junction–Mammoth Highway, 2 miles north of Norris Junction

**Access** - Near the highway

**USGS topographic maps** - Mammoth, Wyoming–Montana; Norris Juntion, Wyoming

**Size** - 16 acres

**Depth** - Average 2 feet, maximum 72 feet

**Elevation** - 7520 feet

**Fish type** - None

For some reason few people venture out to Nymph Lake or walk around its shoreline, even though the lake is about 100 yards from the highway and can be seen easily. Most visitors who stop pull into the turnout beside the lake, casually look Nymph over for a few moments and then drive on. They do not seem to realize that this is a unique lake, with thermal features more like a giant thermal pool than a freshwater lake.

Nymph Lake sits in a small canyon surrounded by gentle, tree-covered slopes. There are several islets on the northwest side of the lake that are made up of organic material, rather than sand or rock. There are deep holes—the deepest measures 72 feet—near the islets created by past thermal activity in the basin. Because of the thermal influences in Nymph Lake, the water temperature is high and the lake is one of the most acidic found in the park. Boiling water from Frying Pan Springs and Roadside Hot Springs, two thermal features along the road just south of the lake, empties into Nymph. The main water source comes from a small, 1-acre pond north of the lake. The outlet, flowing from the south end, empties into the Gibbon River, about 3 miles south.

The thermal features on the north end—between the highway and the lake—and on the northwest and southeast sides are interesting to watch and make Nymph Lake and the small basin fun to explore. The thermal area on the northeast side (to your right as you face the lake from the highway) is located on a sloping hillside, a short way up from the lake. The crust of mineral deposits here, as with all thermal areas, is thin, and the hillside around it is steep. This makes it all too easy to slip and fall and all the more dangerous to get too close.

Fish could migrate from the Gibbon River, up the outlet stream and into Nymph Lake. Given the lake's acidity and high water temperature, however, the fish could not survive.

## 50
# Harlequin Lake

**Location** - Trail on the north side of the Madison Junction–West Yellowstone Highway, 1.6 miles west of Madison Junction

**Access** - Foot trail, .4 mile

**USGS topographic map** - Madison Junction, Wyoming

**Size** - 10 acres

**Depth** - Average 4 feet, maximum 11 feet

**Elevation** - 6890 feet

**Fish type** - None

Harlequin Lake, an enjoyable lake to visit, is on an easy trail only a short distance from the highway and has a pure and natural solitude usually reserved for lakes with no trail access or distant, hard-to-reach lakes. Harlequin is the perfect lake for spending an early morning or late evening watching the wildlife that is almost always present on and around the lake. It's a good place to enjoy a midday picnic in a secluded and natural setting. Not many people visit this lake, for there are no fish in Harlequin.

There is no trailhead marker on the highway, but, if you look closely on the north side of the highway as you drive toward West Yellowstone, you will see an orange trail marker nailed to a tree and the trailhead register nearby. On the op-

*Harlequin Lake*

posite side of the highway is a visitor turnout that overlooks the Madison River. The hike to Harlequin Lake is a short, pleasant one through a lodgepole pine forest on a well-marked trail.

Harlequin is a circular lake nestled into the base of a steep hillside. The south, west and east sides are surrounded by forest; the north end of the lake is a steep, rocky hillside. If you decide to climb around on this end, do it with care. These large boulders appear stable, but are in fact loose and could shift under your weight. The shoreline around a good portion of the west side and all of the north and east sides is wet and marshy.

Harlequin Lake offers 2 vantage points that are ideal for a picnic with a good view of the entire lake and of the wildlife around it. One is the small peninsula on the west end and the other is a small flat area on the northwest hillside, about 50 feet above the lake.

Harlequin Lake's water supply originates from springs that rise to the surface and flow into the lake through channels on the west, north and east ends. There are also underground springs that feed the lake. There are several small outlets on the east end that flow only during periods of high water.

There are no fish in Harlequin Lake and there probably never have been. Its shallow depth and lack of spawning habitat make it an unlikely fishery.

## 51
## Divide
## Lake

**Location** - On the east side of Highway 191, 18.6 miles north of West Yellowstone

**Access** - On the highway

**USGS topographic map** - Tepee Creek, Montana–Wyoming

**Size** - 7 acres

**Depth** - Average 3 feet, maximum 7 feet

**Elevation** - 7239 feet

**Fish type** - None

Divide Lake lies in a flat open meadow along the east side of Highway 191 just east of Yellowstone's western border with Montana. It is a rather small nondescript lake in a remote part of Yellowstone that gets relatively few visitors. Divide Lake usually receives little more than a passing glance from motorists, even though the meadow around the lake is alive with wild strawberries during the summer.

Snowmelt and ground water seepage provide the water for Divide Lake. There is no outlet.

There are no fish in Divide Lake and it's probably safe to say that there have never been any fish in the lake.

# OTHER LAKES TO EXPLORE

## 52
## Shelf
## Lake

**Location** - At the base of Sheep Mountain

**Access** - North Fork of the Specimen Creek Trail, approximately 8 miles

**USGS topographic map** - Crown

Butte, Montana–Wyoming
**Size** - 7 acres
**Depth** - Maximum 40 feet
**Elevation** - 9160 feet
**Fish type** - None

## 53
## Crescent Lake

**Location** - At the headwaters of the North Fork of Specimen Creek
**Access** - Specimen Creek Trail to Crescent Lake Trail, 7 miles
**USGS topographic map** - Miner, Montana–Wyoming
**Size** - 15 acres
**Depth** - Maximum 48 feet
**Elevation** - 8600 feet
**Fish type** - None

*Coyote*

## 54
## Crag
## Lake

**Location** - At the headwaters of the East Fork of Specimen Creek

**Access** - Partial remnants of an old trail, but mainly cross-country travel from Crescent Lake, 8.5 miles

**USGS topographic map** - Miner, Montana–Wyoming

**Size** - 7.5 acres

**Depth** - Maximum 21 feet

**Elevation** - 8800 feet

**Fish type** - None

## 55
## High
## Lake

**Location** - At the headwaters of the East Fork of Specimen Creek

**Access** - Specimen Creek Trailhead to Sportsman Lake Trail to High Lake Trail, 9 miles

**USGS topographic map** - Miner, Montana–Wyoming

**Size** - 7 acres

**Depth** - Maximum 18 feet

**Elevation** - 8774 feet

**Fish type** - Cutthroat trout

## 56
## Sportsman
## Lake

**Location** - In the Gallatin Range west of Mol Heron Creek

**Access** - Sportsman Lake Trail, 13 miles; Specimen Creek Trail, 11 miles

**USGS topographic map** - Miner, Montana–Wyoming

**Size** - 4 acres

**Depth** - Average 5 feet, maximum 26 feet

**Elevation** - 7730 feet

**Fish type** - Cutthroat trout

## 57
## Cache
## Lake

**Location** - In the Gallatin Range west of Mammoth Hot Springs

**Access** - Sportsman–Cache Lake trails, 6 miles

**USGS topographic map** - Mt. Holmes, Wyoming–Montana

**Size** - 16 acres

**Depth** - Average 4 feet, maximum 12 feet

**Elevation** - 8050 feet

**Fish type** - None

## 58
## Rainbow
## Lakes

**Location** - 1.5 miles southwest of Gardiner, Montana

**Access** - 1 mile northwest of Gardiner, Montana, along the Gardiner–Cinnabar Road, then 1.5 miles south on an old abandoned road

**USGS topographic map** - Gardiner, Montana

**Sizes** - Upper lake 1.5 acres, middle lake 3.5 acres, lower lake 1.5 acres

**Depths** - Upper lake unsurveyed, generally shallow; middle lake average 3 feet, maximum 9 feet; lower lake unsurveyed

**Elevation** - 5880 feet

**Fish type** - None

## 59
## Mammoth Beaver Ponds

**Location** - Northwest of Mammoth Hot Springs

**Access** - Beaver Ponds Loop Trail, 2.5 miles

**USGS topographic map** - Mammoth, Wyoming– Montana

**Sizes** - Large Mammoth Beaver Pond 10 acres, Little Mammoth Beaver Pond 2 acres

**Depths** - Large Mammoth Beaver Pond average 6 feet, maximum 13 feet; Little Mammoth Beaver Pond average 9 feet, maximum 18 feet

**Elevations** - Large Mammoth Beaver Pond 6320 feet, Little Mammoth Beaver Pond 6520 feet

**Fish type** - None

## 60
## Fawn Lake

**Location** - North end of Gardner's Hole, south of Fawn Pass Trail

**Access** - Glen Creek Trail to Fawn Pass Trail, approximately 5 miles

**USGS topographic map** - Mt. Holmes, Wyoming– Montana

**Size** - 5 acres

**Depth** - Average 8 feet, maximum 18 feet

**Elevation** - 7800 feet

**Fish type** - Brook trout

## 61
## Gallatin Lake

**Location** - At the headwaters of the Gallatin River

**Access** - Bighorn Pass Trail to the Gallatin River, then follow the river upstream to Gallatin Lake, approximately 10 miles

**USGS topographic map** - Mt. Holmes, Wyoming–Montana

**Size** - 19.5 acres

**Depth** - Maximum 47 feet

**Elevation** - 8834 feet

**Fish type** - None

## 62
## Trilobite Lake

**Location** - In the Gallatin Range between Mt. Holmes and Dome Mountain

**Access** - Winter Creek (Mt. Holmes) Trail to Winter Creek patrol cabin, approximately 6 miles, then north on an unmaintained trail, approximately 3 miles

**USGS topographic map** - Mt. Holmes, Wyoming–Montana

**Size** - 11 acres

**Depth** - Average 21 feet, maximum 43 feet

**Elevation** - 8366 feet

**Fish type** - Brook trout

*Lake of the Woods*

# Washburn Region

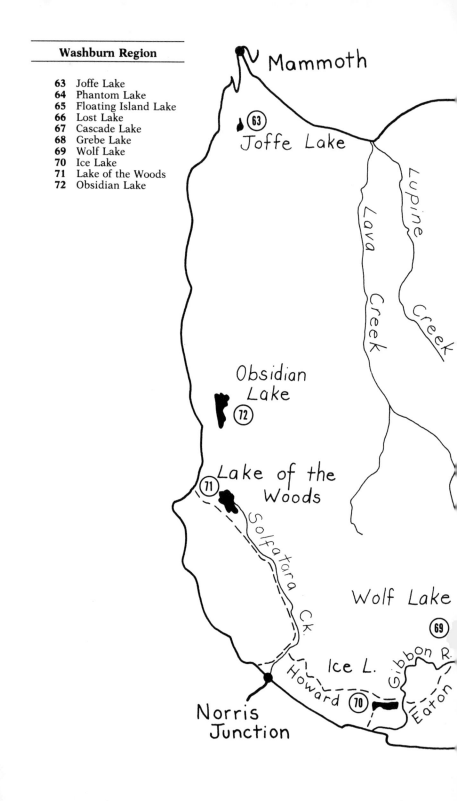

## Washburn Region

Mammoth

63 Joffe Lake

Lava Creek

Lupine Creek

Obsidian Lake 72

71 Lake of the Woods

Solfatara Ck.

Wolf Lake 69

Ice L.

Gibbon R.

Eaton

Howard 70

Norris Junction

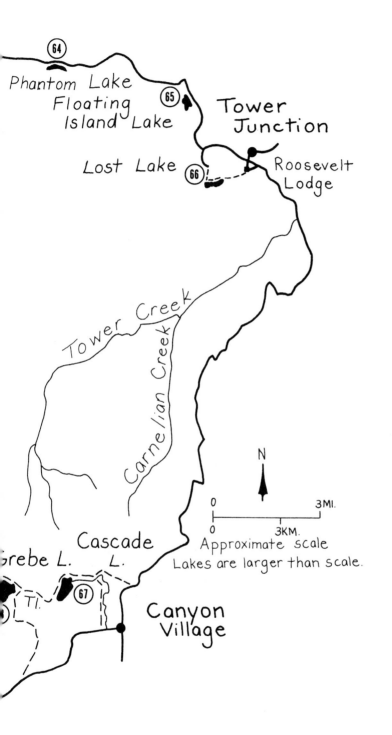

64

Phantom Lake
Floating
Island Lake

65

Tower
Junction

Lost Lake 66

Roosevelt
Lodge

Tower Creek

Carnelian Creek

N

0               3MI.

0       3KM.
Approximate scale
Lakes are larger than scale.

Cascade
Grebe L.    L.

Tl.

67

Canyon
Village

# 63
## Joffe
## Lake

**Location** - At the end of a dirt road that turns off the east side of the Mammoth–Norris Highway, 1.2 miles south of Mammoth

**Access** - Dirt road, .9 mile

**USGS topographic map** - Mammoth, Wyoming–Montana

**Size** - 1.5 acres

**Depth** - Maximum 9 feet

**Elevation** - 6500 feet

**Fish type** - Brook trout

Joffe Lake is a pleasant little lake, a good spot to take younger children who are just learning how to fish. The small brook trout in Joffe seem hyperactive; they are constantly rising to the surface and jumping. You begin to think that they are simply having a good time, rather than feeding on insects. The brookies are not difficult to catch and this presents a good opportunity for young fishermen, anxious to try their luck with flies and small spinners.

Although the drive to the lake takes a little figuring out, Joffe Lake offers seclusion and a pleasant area to picnic and relax while your kids are fishing. At 1.2 miles south of Mammoth, you will see a road on your left. Turn here and follow the truck route to the left and around the residential area. At the maintenance yard, veer to the left and, at the fork in the road, head left again. This will take you to the end of the road and Joffe Lake. It is .9 mile from the turnoff at the highway to the lake.

Joffe Lake lies in a small depression on the north side and at the base of 8564-foot Bunsen Peak. (The large rock formation you see about half way up Bunsen Peak to the southwest is Cathedral Rock.) The lake is easy to get around, although it is somewhat wet on the east end.

The water supply to Joffe Lake comes from the Mammoth Water Supply Reservoir, about a quarter of a mile northwest of the lake. Mammoth Reservoir's water supply is furnished by a man-made diversion on Glen Creek. Water enters Joffe

*Joffe Lake*

Lake through an inlet stream at the southwestern end of the lake. The outlet, on the southeast side, of Joffe is a 50-foot pipe through an earth-fill dam. The water flows only a short distance before reentering Glen Creek.

*Phantom Lake*

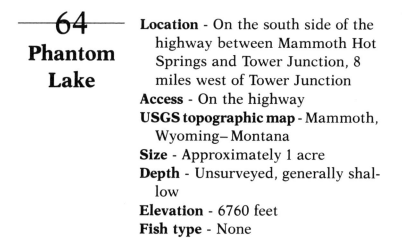

## 64
## Phantom Lake

**Location** - On the south side of the highway between Mammoth Hot Springs and Tower Junction, 8 miles west of Tower Junction

**Access** - On the highway

**USGS topographic map** - Mammoth, Wyoming–Montana

**Size** - Approximately 1 acre

**Depth** - Unsurveyed, generally shallow

**Elevation** - 6760 feet

**Fish type** - None

Phantom Lake is a small, shallow roadside lake, pretty in the spring, full of frogs and aquatic insects. By midsummer the water level subsides, Phantom Lake disappears, and the lake basin is covered with thick grass and vegetation. Oxbow Creek, a tributary of the Yellowstone River, flows from the base of 9625-foot Prospect Peak, southeast of Phantom Lake, gathering water from snowmelt during the spring runoff and depositing it in the small basin that becomes Phantom Lake. By late spring, however, water no longer runs in the creek and the lake begins to dry up.

## 65
## Floating Island Lake

**Location** - On the south side of the Mammoth–Tower Junction Highway, 3.4 miles west of Tower Junction

**Access** - On the highway

**USGS topographic map** - Tower Junction, Wyoming–Montana

**Size** - 5.8 acres

**Depth** - Maximum 10 feet

**Elevation** - 6500 feet

**Fish type** - None

*Floating Island Lake*

Floating Island Lake lies alongside the highway. There is a vehicle turnout at the lake and plenty of room for visitors to park. Floating Island gets its fair share of visitors simply because it is a pretty lake and easy to get to, although most people stop for a few minutes and see what they can without getting out of their cars. The lake is in fact worth the time it takes to get out and walk around.

As the name indicates, there is an island, composed of organic vegetation, at the northwest end of the lake. The meadows surrounding the lake are loaded with bird life and the lake attracts a good quantity and variety of ducks, such as lesser scaup, Barrow's goldeneye and ruddy ducks. One of the most interesting birds you will find here is the yellow-headed blackbird, the only bird in North America that has a yellow head and a black body. The males' cry, a long and rather harsh buzzing sound, lasts for several seconds and is unmistakable. The females are a brownish color with a yellow throat.

Floating Island Lake lies in a glacial depression at the base of Crescent Hill. It is ringed with bulrushes and the area immediately around the lake is open and grassy. The walk around the lake is on solid ground, except in the spring and early summer, when the west end can be marshy.

There are no fish in Floating Island Lake and no records to indicate that it has ever been stocked. Because of its shallow depth and lack of an inlet and an outlet stream, the lake has probably never supported fish. Its water source is from underground springs that flow into the dry channel on the southwest end of the lake.

## 66
## Lost
## Lake

**Location** - Near Tower Junction

**Access** - Lost Lake Trail, .5 mile from the trailhead at the petrified tree or 1.5 miles from Roosevelt Lodge

**USGS topographic map** - Tower Junction, Wyoming–Montana

**Size** - 6 acres

**Depth** - Average 18 feet, maximum 41 feet

**Elevation** - 6760 feet

**Fish type** - None

Lost Lake, near Tower Junction, is 1 of 3 Lost Lakes in Yellowstone. The second is located near Mammoth and the third is in fact "lost." Early maps of Yellowstone showed a lake between Shoshone Lake and the West Thumb of Yellowstone Lake. Despite efforts to find it, that Lost Lake's location remains a mystery.

You can walk to Lost Lake from the trailhead behind Roosevelt Lodge near Tower Junction or from the trailhead at the petrified tree, less than 2 miles west of Tower Junction. From Roosevelt Lodge it's 1.5 miles to the lake and from the petrified tree, .5 mile.

Lost Lake is long and narrow, situated in a small, deep draw. It is a beautiful lake, ringed with yellow pond lilies and usually covered with ducks. The meadow on the west end, where the inlet stream is located, is full of wildflowers. Clusters of alpine forget-me-nots, small, delicate blue flowers with a yellow center, are found near Lost Lake, especially along the trail and near the base of the hillsides. There is a beaver lodge and dam near the outlet on the east end. Downed and partially eaten trees around the lake are evidence that the beavers here are quite active. Steep, tree-covered hillsides border the lake on the north and south ends, but the walk along the trail on the north side of the lake is easy. Because of the steep hillside, the trees that grow almost to the shoreline and the absence of a trail, walking around the south end is somewhat difficult.

Originally Lost Lake was barren. In 1933, 6000 rainbow trout were planted in the lake, followed by another 4500 trout in 1934. Lost Lake is barren again, however, because it lacks suitable spawning habitat.

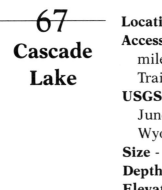

## 67
## Cascade Lake

**Location** - Near Canyon Village

**Access** - Cascade Lake Trail, 2.5 miles; Cascade Lake Picnic Area Trail, 2.5 miles

**USGS topographic maps** - Norris Junction, Wyoming; Mammoth, Wyoming– Montana

**Size** - 36 acres

**Depth** - Maximum 27 feet

**Elevation** - 7980 feet

**Fish types** - Cutthroat trout, grayling

There are 2 trailheads to Cascade Lake. The Cascade Lake trailhead is .5 mile west of Canyon Village on the north side of the Canyon–Norris Highway. The Cascade Lake picnic area trailhead is 1.25 miles north of Canyon Village on the west side of the Canyon–Tower Highway. Both trailheads mark 2.5-mile routes to Cascade Lake, easy walks through lodge-

*Above: Alpine forget-me-nots. Below: Cascade Lake Trail through meadow just before reaching Cascade Lake*

*Grebe Lake*

pole pine forests and open meadows on flat and well-defined trails. Both trails come together a mile or so east of Cascade Lake. At the lake, the trail joins the Howard Eaton Trail on the northwest end and continues on to Grebe, Wolf and Ice lakes.

The possibility of seeing moose along the trails is good and so is your chance of spotting a grizzly. When hiking in this area, you should always check with the backcountry office at Canyon Village. In the Canyon area, they often recommend that you hike in parties of 4 or more, for this part of the Solfatara Plateau is a high bear-use area.

Cascade Lake lies in a natural depression at the base of Observation Peak. The lake is bordered by a large grassy meadow on the north end, where you first come upon the lake, and a dense forest borders the shoreline on the east side. The wooded area is usually wet and there are numerous downfalls that make getting around the east side difficult. The meadow at the south end is wet and boggy, but you can pick your way through it without getting wet. Cascade Lake's west side is a meadowy hillside that extends back from the lake about 200 feet before turning into a dense wood.

The water supply for Cascade Lake comes from a stream that enters the lake on the south end and from springs and

seepage on the south and east slopes. The outlet on the north
end is Cascade Creek, a tributary of the Yellowstone River.

Although it was once a barren lake, Cascade contains a
good population of cutthroat trout. It's one of the few lakes in
the park—and the only lake in the Yellowstone River drainage—that contains grayling. Records indicate that there may
have been an unofficial stocking of 50 cutthroat trout from
Yellowstone Lake in 1889. Cascade Creek was stocked with
cutthroats in 1901, 1922 and 1925 and those efforts would account for the cutthroat trout in Cascade Lake today. From
1933 to 1943 and from 1949 to 1955, Cascade Lake received
annual stockings of grayling from the hatchery at Grebe Lake.

## 68
## Grebe
## Lake

**Location** - Near Canyon Village
**Access** - Foot trail, 3 miles
**USGS topographic maps** - Norris
Junction, Wyoming; Mammoth,
Wyoming–Montana
**Size** - 156 acres
**Depth** - Maximum 32 feet
**Elevation** - 8000 feet
**Fish types** - Grayling, rainbow trout

A trailhead sign on the highway indicates the turn into the
parking area at the Grebe Lake trailhead on the north side of
the highway, 3.4 miles west of Canyon Village. Grebe Lake is a
popular area for both day use and overnight camping.

The hike to Grebe Lake is an easy one through a lodgepole
pine forest, on a flat and well-defined trail. If you don't stop,
it takes about an hour to reach the lake. The beginning of the
trail is an old road that was used when the Bureau of Fisheries established a fish hatchery at Grebe Lake in 1933. The
hatchery was closed in the mid-1950s and so was the road.
For the first half mile or so, hikers on the trail will be pestered
by clouds of mosquitoes until the late summer. Grizzlies are
often seen in this area of the Solfatara Plateau and it's a good

idea to have 2 or 3 other hikers with you when walking to Grebe or any other lake in this area. If you go alone, stay alert and make plenty of noise. It is also worthwhile to check at the Canyon Village Ranger Station for reports on any recent bear activity.

Grebe Lake is circular and surrounded by meadows, except at the southwest end, where the forest borders the shoreline. It's easy to walk around the lake on good solid ground, except at the west and southwest ends, which are marshy. These are also good areas in which to see moose.

Grebe Lake's water supply originates in spring-fed inlets on the north and east sides. Grebe Lake is the headwater of the Gibbon River, the lake's only outlet. The spawning habitat is adequate in the outlet and all of the inlets.

Because barriers in the lower part of the Gibbon River prevented upstream fish migration, the whole upper Gibbon River system—which includes Ice, Wolf and Grebe lakes—was originally barren. Initial fish stocking in the upper Gibbon River system began in 1907, with plants of rainbow trout eggs in Grebe Lake. In 1912, 300,000 Yellowstone Lake cutthroat trout fry were stocked in Grebe Lake and a million grayling eggs from the Montana state hatchery at Anaconda were planted in 1921. After the fish hatchery was established at Grebe Lake in 1933, grayling were stocked on a regular basis until the last plants were made in 1956, after the hatchery closed. By the early 1950s all of the trout in Grebe Lake were considered to be hybrid crosses between rainbows and cutthroats. The outward appearance of the fish was that of a rainbow trout, but it had a red slash on the outside of the lower jaw and teeth, called hyoid teeth, at the base of the tongue, a characteristic of cutthroat trout. By 1969 the trout exhibited rainbow characteristics only and most of the trout now in Grebe Lake are rainbows.

With sufficient spawning habitat, both grayling and rainbow trout have been successful in reproducing, and both species are in excellent condition. The grayling population outnumbers that of the rainbow, a factor explained by the ease with which grayling are caught and the regulation that fishing for grayling is catch and release only. All grayling must be returned to Grebe Lake.

## 69
## Wolf
## Lake

**Location** - Near Canyon Village
**Access** - Ice Lake Trail, 4 miles;
Grebe Lake Trail, 5 miles; Cascade
Lake Trail, 6.5 miles; Cascade
Lake Picnic Area Trail, 6.5 miles
**USGS topographic map** - Norris
Junction, Wyoming
**Size** - 51 acres
**Depth** - Maximum 32 feet
**Elevation** - 7998 feet
**Fish types** - Rainbow trout, grayling

You can walk to Wolf Lake from 4 separate trailheads. All of the trails are flat and offer easy walking through meadows and dense lodgepole pine.

The Ice Lake Trailhead, 4 miles from Wolf Lake, is on the

*Wolf Lake*

north side of the Canyon–Norris Highway, 3.3 miles east of Norris Junction. (The Ice Lake Trail joins the Howard Eaton Trail on the northwest side of Ice Lake and continues along the north side of the lake for about half a mile before continuing on to Wolf Lake.) On the Ice Lake Trail, you will have to ford the Gibbon River a couple of times before reaching Wolf Lake.

The Grebe Lake Trailhead, 5 miles from Wolf Lake, is on the north side of the Canyon–Norris Highway, 3.4 miles west of Canyon Village. This trail is actually the old fish hatchery road. At Grebe Lake, 2 miles from Wolf Lake, you can walk around the east side of the lake and join the Howard Eaton Trail, which runs through the meadow on the northeast end. As you enter the second large meadow after leaving Grebe Lake you will be able to see Wolf Lake on your right, about 200 yards from the trail.

Wolf Lake can also be reached by joining the Howard Eaton Trail on the northwest end of Cascade Lake. From either Cascade Lake trailhead it is 6.5 miles to Wolf Lake.

Grizzlies are often seen in this area of the Solfatara Plateau and it's a good idea to stay alert, make plenty of noise and not hike alone. It is also worthwhile to check at the Canyon Village Ranger Station for reports of recent bear activity.

A large meadow borders Wolf Lake's northwest and southeast shores, and lodgepole pine rim the northeast and southwest ends of the lake. This combination of woods, meadows and water is particularly attractive to moose, which are often seen around the lake. Wolf's main water supply is the Gibbon River, which flows out of nearby Grebe Lake and into the east side of Wolf Lake. The inlet's concentration of good spawning gravel provides the primary spawning habitat for both rainbow trout and grayling. Additional water sources are 2 small streams that enter the northwest end of the lake, groundwater seepage and a number of small springs around the lake. The only outlet is the Gibbon River, which flows from the southeast end of Wolf Lake and meanders in a southwesterly direction for about 25 miles before it joins the Firehole River to form the Madison River.

Because Wolf Lake is fed by the Gibbon River, which flows out of Grebe Lake, its history of fish stocking is shared with

Grebe Lake. Barriers in the lower part of the Gibbon River prevented fish from migrating upstream, so the whole upper Gibbon River system (which includes Ice, Wolf and Grebe lakes) was originally barren. Rainbow trout eggs were planted in Grebe Lake in 1907, Yellowstone Lake cutthroat fry were released in 1912 and grayling eggs in 1921. After the fish hatchery was established at Grebe Lake in 1933, grayling were stocked in Wolf Lake on a regular basis until 1956. By the early 1950s, all trout in Grebe and Wolf lakes were hybrid crosses of rainbows and cutthroats. By 1969 the trout found in Wolf and Grebe lakes had only rainbow trout characteristics.

# 70
## Ice
## Lake

**Location** - Near Norris Junction
**Access** - Ice Lake Trail, .2 mile
**USGS topographic map** - Norris
   Junction, Wyoming
**Size** - 224 acres
**Depth** - Average 22 feet, maximum
   53 feet
**Elevation** - 7880 feet
**Fish type** - None

The Ice Lake Trailhead is located on the north side of the Norris–Canyon Highway, 3.3 miles east of Norris Junction. The sign at the trailhead says that it is .5 mile to the lake and, you no sooner start off for Ice Lake, when, suddenly, you're there. It takes 5 minutes to reach the western end of the lake. The trail continues along the west side and joins the Howard Eaton Trail at the northwest end of the lake. The Howard Eaton Trail follows the north shore for a little over .5 mile before leaving Ice Lake and continuing to Wolf, Grebe and Cascade lakes.

Completely surrounded by a dense lodgepole pine forest, Ice Lake is a long, narrow lake on the Solfatara Plateau. The area around the lake is fairly flat and takes only about an hour to make the easy circuit.

Seepage and underground springs provide the water for Ice

*Ice Lake*

Lake. There is a small low gradient outlet stream on the eastern tip that empties into the nearby Gibbon River.

It's almost unbelievable but Ice Lake, after being stocked with 3.8 million fish over a period spanning 56 years, is barren again today. Between 1905 and 1961, 3.4 million grayling were planted in the lake. It was also stocked with 11,000 brook trout in 1905, 389,000 cutthroats between 1930 and 1936 and 4000 rainbow trout in 1943. A few grayling—the results of partially successful spawning in the 1961 grayling plants—were found in the lake in 1969. Although a great effort was made to keep fish in Ice Lake, the lack of a constantly flowing inlet and outlet has caused poor spawning conditions and Ice Lake is unable to provide for a self-sustaining fish population.

## 71
# Lake of the Woods

**Location** - Trailhead on the east side of the Mammoth– Norris Highway, 7.3 miles north of Norris Junction, .3 mile south of Beaver Lake

*Possibly a bear-clawed tree (notice claw marks below scrape)*

**Access** - Foot trail and off-trail travel, 1.5 miles

**USGS topographic map** - Mammoth, Wyoming–Montana

**Size** - 26 acres

**Depth** - Average 6 feet, maximum 23 feet

**Elevation** - 7700 feet

**Fish type** - None

Getting to Lake of the Woods takes some effort and the use of a compass and the Mammoth, Wyoming–Montana, 15-minute topographic map. Even the trailhead is difficult to find. There is a small, narrow road on the east side of the highway, 7.3 miles north of Norris Junction and just south of Beaver Lake. You have to look carefully because the road is bordered by dense forest and is easy to miss. Once you make the turn it is a very short distance to the end of the road and the Whiterock Springs and Solfatara Creek trailhead. The trail eventually joins the Howard Eaton Trail just north of the Norris Campground.

Most people who try to visit Lake of the Woods never reach it because the lake can't be seen from the trail. During the late 1800s and early 1900s, the main road passed near the lake and travelers visited it often. Since the road was rerouted, Lake of the Woods rarely has visitors. To reach it you must leave the trail after a little more than a mile and bushwhack for about .2 mile through dense forest.

The trail starts out flat and easy to follow. You will quickly pass a small stream called Lemonade Creek. Its emeraldlike color comes from green algae growing in the creek bottom. After the first 150 yards or so, the trail bears left and climbs steeply over a small, grassy hill. The trail is not well defined here, but if you look up the grassy hill to your left, you will see an orange trail marker nailed to a post. This is where you should climb the hill. From the top of the hill, the trail is hidden by fallen trees. Again, look for the orange trail markers. They will help keep you on the trail. When you get through this section, you will find that the trail is, once again, well defined and easy to follow. The hot springs you see below the trail is Amphitheater Springs, the water source for Lemonade Creek. After a steady climb the trail goes under a powerline, through a wide cut in the otherwise thick lodgepole pine. Near this point you leave the trail and walk northwest .2 mile through dense forest to the lake. You can reach Lake of the Woods safely and successfully and find your way out again only by having and knowing how to use a compass and the topographic map. Even if you have a good sense of direction, the dense forest and the lack of prominent landmarks make it necessary for you to use a compass to ensure that you're going in the right direction.

You will come upon the lake along its northwest or west side, and you will not see Lake of the Woods until you are almost there because it is completely surrounded by lodgepole pine. The setting is very secluded and you will more than likely have the lake all to yourself. The shoreline is a little marshy but you can get around the lake without any problems. There is a meadow on the east side, where the outlet is located, and a small pond at the back of the meadow near the trees. The lake is ringed with yellow pond lilies and wildflowers grow around the lake. Wild strawberries are plentiful during the summer.

There are usually Barrow's goldeneye, as well as other ducks, on the lake and the number of game trails around it indicate that Lake of the Woods is an important water source for the area's wildlife. About 75 feet from the lake on the small hill on the east side, there are several trees with claw marks that were probably left by a bear. Bears like to rub and scratch themselves on pine and fir trees and, while doing so, will often reach up and scratch the tree. Sometimes bears will claw and chew on pine, spruce and fir trees to get the sap that is just beneath the bark. Badgers and bobcats will also claw trees.

The water sources for Lake of the Woods are snowmelt and runoff. There are no inlets or known springs that feed the lake. The outlet on the east side flows into Whiterock Springs and Solfatara Creek.

Local fishermen believe that brook and cutthroat trout were once planted in Lake of the Woods, but there are no records to show that this was actually done. Records do indicate that 5000 rainbow trout were stocked in 1937. With no spawning habitat, however, Lake of the Woods soon returned to its original barren state.

# 72
# Obsidian Lake

**Location** - On the east side of the Norris Junction–Mammoth Highway, 9.3 miles north of Norris Junction

**Access** - Off-trail travel, .7 mile

**USGS topographic map** - Mammoth, Wyoming–Montana

**Size** - 28 acres

**Depth** - Average 4 feet, maximum 25 feet

**Elevation** - 7759 feet

**Fish type** - None

If you hike to Obsidian Lake, you can be assured of quiet solitude in a pristine environment. Although less than a mile from the highway, the lake has no trail to lead to it and you

*Obsidian Lake*

must climb a very steep hill, cross through a draw, over a ridge and down to the lake.

The starting point for Obsidian Lake is directly across the highway from the Winter Creek trailhead, which is also called the Mt. Holmes Trail. The vehicle parking area for the Winter Creek trailhead is on the west side of the highway, 9.3 miles north of Norris Junction and .3 mile south of Apollinaris Springs. Hiking to Obsidian Lake can be done safely only with the use of a compass and the Mammoth, Wyoming–Montana, 15-minute topographic map. At the start locate your exact position on the topographic map and take note of the compass bearing that you must follow all the way to the lake. Trust your compass and go in the exact direction that it tells you.

Once you leave the highway, you enter a heavy forest and will have to pick your way through downfall for about 100 yards, until you reach Obsidian Creek. After you cross the creek, you'll climb a steep hill, about .2 mile from the highway. At the top of the hill, you cross through a shallow draw filled with lodgepole pine and pass over a small ridge before dropping down to Obsidian Lake. You can catch a welcome glimpse of the lake about 150 feet before you get there.

Obsidian Lake is long and narrow, scattered with yellow pond lilies and ringed by a narrow sedge-grass meadow. There are 2 beaver lodges on the southwest end and signs of beaver-cut trees along the western edge. Ducks, sandpipers and other birds are abundant and so are the well-traveled game trails that wind through the small basin around the lake. Like Lake of the Woods, 2 miles to the south, Obsidian Lake is an important source of water for the area's wildlife.

Obsidian Lake has neither an inlet nor an outlet stream. Its main water supply comes from underground springs and, to a lesser extent, spring snowmelt. There are no fish in the lake and probably never have been.

Because it is secluded, barren and difficult to reach, Obsidian Lake is seldom visited. This isolation offers the cross-country hiker a wonderful opportunity to experience and photograph one of the most tranquil and pristine lakes found in Yellowstone.

*Shrimp Lake*

# North Region

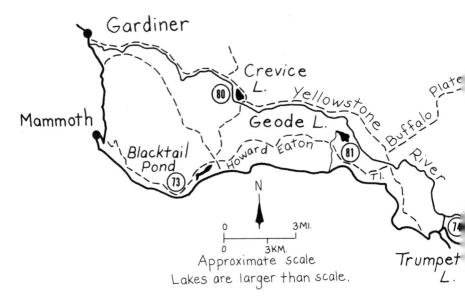

Approximate scale
Lakes are larger than scale.

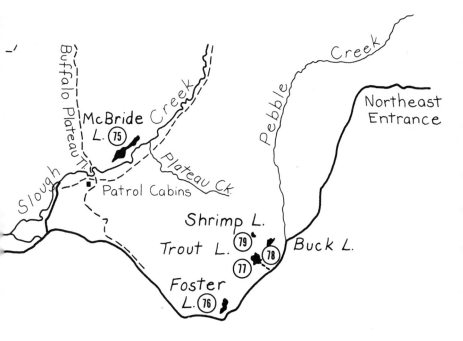

# —73—
# Blacktail Pond

**Location** - On the north side of the highway between Mammoth Hot Springs and Tower Junction, 6 miles east of Mammoth Hot Springs

**Access** - Near the highway

**USGS topographic map** - Mammoth, Wyoming–Montana

**Size** - 11 acres

**Depth** - Average 11 feet, maximum 26 feet

**Elevation** - 6600 feet

**Fish types** - Cutthroat, brook trout

Blacktail Pond lies in an open sagebrush and sedge grass covered glacial basin about 150 yards from the highway. There is a vehicle turnout on the highway at the lake and, although the lake may not look very interesting, it is worth the time it takes to visit. From the turnout there is an easy trail leading down to the lake. Once you're there you'll know why Blacktail Pond is known locally as Shakey Lake.

Dense masses of aquatic vegetation have matted over, forming a wet, spongy, groundlike surface that feels as though you're walking on a trampoline. The older part of the sedge mat is solid and fairly stable, but it is unstable near the edge. The walking surface along the south shoreline and the western end is bouncy but stable, if you're careful and go easy. It is a good idea to wear waterproof boots or hip boots, because there are spots that are almost always wet. Walking around the shoreline on the north and east sides is difficult at best, especially in the spring and early summer. The vegetation is sparse and you'll have to walk through soft muck and mud.

Blacktail Pond's water supply comes from underground springs beneath the lake and from a small stream that flows into the lake on the southwestern end from a spring several hundred feet away. The outlet stream on the northeast end

*Blacktail Pond*

flows for about 1 mile before emptying into Blacktail Deer Creek.

It is not known when brook trout first appeared in Blacktail Pond. Between 1909 and 1943, 149,890 brook trout, 695,000 cutthroats and 3000 rainbow trout were planted in nearby Blacktail Deer Creek. The brook trout could have entered Blacktail Pond via the outlet, which connects with Blacktail Deer Creek. The cutthroats and rainbow trout could have done the same thing. Although a stream's shallow depth and low flow restrain fish movement, Blacktail Deer Creek doesn't have any barriers to migration.

Blacktail Pond was stocked with 10,500 brook trout in 1939. Between 1939 and 1957, 27,900 cutthroat trout and 53 cutthroat–rainbow hybrids were planted. During a Fish and Wildlife Service survey conducted in 1966, only brook trout were found in the lake. In an attempt to restore the cutthroat population, 200 cutthroats from Bear Creek, an inlet to Turbid Lake, were planted in Blacktail Pond in 1980 and another 270 in 1982.

Blacktail Pond is a nutrient-rich environment, capable of supporting one of the highest quality fisheries in Yellowstone. The cutthroats, however, have never been able to sustain themselves in Blacktail Pond because of its limited spawning habitat and the fish may eventually disappear. Cutthroats must have the flowing water of an inlet or outlet stream to reproduce successfully. Brook trout, in comparison, can successfully spawn by using areas of upswelling, springs and seeps within the lake itself, if inlets or outlets are not available. The brook trout in Blacktail Pond are abundant, in excellent condition and of an above-average size for lakes in Yellowstone.

Blacktail Pond is a popular fishery—it ranks third in angler use. In addition to its easy access, a major factor that might contribute to its popularity is the sign at the turnout on the highway, which states, "Catch and release fishing only for Yellowstone native cutthroat trout." To a fisherman, this sign might indicate that there is a good population of cutthroats in this lake—and some sizeable ones as well. The productive environment of Blacktail Pond and the great reproductive success of the adaptable and prolific brook trout have maintained a quality fishery, even though this species receives excessive fishing pressure and harvest.

## 74
## Trumpeter Lakes

**Location** - On the north side of the Northeast Entrance Highway, 2.5 miles east of Tower Junction

**Access** - Off-trail travel, .3 mile

**USGS topographic map** - Tower Junction, Wyoming–Montana

**Sizes** - Trumpeter Lake 26 acres, Little Trumpeter Lake 10 acres

**Depths** - Trumpeter Lake average 5 feet, maximum 10 feet; Little Trumpeter Lake average 7 feet, maximum 10 feet

**Elevations** - Trumpeter Lake 6145 feet, Little Trumpeter Lake 6110 feet

**Fish type** - None

The Trumpeter Lakes are typical of the many glacial lakes found throughout the Lamar Valley. They are unnamed on topographic maps and, though somewhat larger, might be confused with other lakes in the immediate area. The glacier that carved and sliced its way through the northeastern part of Yellowstone National Park some 10,000 to 11,000 years ago pulled rocks and large boulders from the mountainsides as it crept down, and formed, the Lamar Valley.

These rocks and boulders became the tools that dug and gouged small, shallow basins in the valley floor. In the places where the landscape provided water to these basins, a glacial lake was formed. The rocks and boulders that remained after the glacier melted, called erratics, can be seen scattered throughout the Lamar Valley.

On the north side of the Northeast Entrance Highway, 2.5 miles east of Tower Junction, there is a vehicle turnout where you can park to hike across treeless and gently rolling hills the .3 mile to Trumpeter Lakes. The two lakes are about 100 yards apart; Little Trumpeter Lake lies to the west and Trumpeter Lake to the east. The Lamar River flows through a narrow canyon several hundred yards north of the lakes and 6598-foot Junction Butte lies just west of Little Trumpeter Lake. The Trumpeter Lakes are seldom visited because they do not contain fish and they are just barely visible from the highway.

The immediate area around the lakes is marshy. Sedges border the lakes and bulrushes and cattails grow in the shallow areas. This type of environment almost always means abundant wildlife. Yellow-headed and red-winged blackbirds are common, as are ducks on the lake and shorebirds such as avocets, killdeers and phalaropes, the small birds that spin in circles in shallow water hoping to stir up food and insect larvae. There is also a good likelihood that you'll see a hawk.

*Unnamed glacial lake in the Lamar Valley*

*McBride Lake*

# 75
## McBride Lake

**Location** - Trailhead on the Slough Creek Campground Road, 1.7 miles from the turnoff of the Northeast Entrance Highway

**Access** - Foot trail and off-trail travel, 3 miles

**USGS topographic maps** - Tower Junction, Wyoming– Montana; Abiathar Peak, Wyoming– Montana

**Size** - 23 acres

**Depth** - Maximum 22 feet

**Elevation** - 6560 feet

**Fish type** - Cutthroat trout

McBride Lake is without a doubt one of the most beautiful backcountry lakes in Yellowstone. It's hidden in a narrow gorge, between high rock walls that reach over 100 feet above the lake's southeast shoreline. From McBride's southwest end, the view of 10,691-foot Cutoff Mountain is one of the most magnificent in Yellowstone. There is no marked trail leading to McBride, hikers have to ford Slough Creek. The Slough Creek Valley and the area around McBride Lake is used by grizzlies throughout the summer. Backcountry camping is not allowed at times. Grizzlies are often sighted in this part of Yellowstone and it is well worth the effort to check at the ranger station at Tower Junction to see if there has been recent sightings.

The trailhead for McBride Lake is on the Slough Creek Campground Road, 5.7 miles northeast of Tower Junction. The 11-mile Slough Creek Trail is an old wagon road still used today by horse-drawn wagons to carry supplies to the privately owned Silvertip Ranch on Yellowstone's northern border. For the first 2 miles, the trail climbs gradually through a forest of Douglas fir until it reaches the banks of Slough Creek, where the forest gives way to a wide, grassy meadow. The trail passes National Park Service patrol cabins and leads away from Slough Creek for about half a mile, then curves to the right and starts to climb. This is the point where you need your topographic map to leave the trail, walk across the meadow and down to Slough Creek, skirting the bottom of the hill to your right. You should come upon Slough Creek at the end of the meadow, where the stream flows through a small, narrow tree-lined canyon. There is usually a good place to ford the creek downstream, but you must judge the safety factor for yourself. Slough Creek's current can be swift and the cold water deep. The water level doesn't usually subside enough for Slough Creek to be forded safely until July.

After you cross Slough Creek, you have two choices for the last .3 mile to McBride. You can climb the rocky hillside in front of you to your right and cross over the top to the edge of a cliff, where you will have a splendid view of the lake. From this point, however, it is a steep and dangerous climb down to the lake. Or you can ford Slough Creek, head around the base of the hill and then angle off to the right, following a wide draw through the trees. You will approach the lake at the southwestern end, which gives you that gorgeous view of McBride Lake with Cutoff Mountain in the background.

Getting around the lake is not difficult. There are places, however, where high rock walls border the shoreline, and you will be forced to hike around them. The area on the northeast end of the lake opens up to form a large meadow that often holds elk and moose. Because McBride Lake receives heavy use from hikers and is located in bear country, camping is not allowed anywhere around the lake. The closest backcountry campsite is at Plateau Creek, more than a mile past the point where you left the trail to ford Slough Creek.

Cutthroat trout are native to McBride Lake. They migrated up Slough Creek, which is a tributary of the Yellowstone River, the source of the first cutthroats to enter Yellowstone. From Slough Creek, the trout found their way into the lake by swimming up the major outlet stream, which flows from the northeast corner of McBride Lake. Another outlet flows from the southwest end, but the volume of water is low, even during the high-water periods in the spring. This outlet widens out and the water dissipates into a marshy area north of Slough Creek. The water supply to McBride Lake comes from an inlet stream at the northwest corner and from springs within the lake.

## 76
## Foster Lake

**Location** - On the north side of the Northeast Entrance Highway, 14.5 miles east of Tower Junction

**Access** - Off-trail travel, .3 mile

**USGS topographic map** - Abiathar Peak, Wyoming–Montana

**Size** - 8 acres

**Depth** - Average 9 feet, maximum 19 feet

**Elevation** - 6620 feet

**Fish type** - None

Foster Lake appears as an unnamed lake on topographic maps, but it is the only lake in the immediate area. Although

*Foster Lake*

just .3 mile north of the Northeast Entrance Highway, Foster Lake can't be seen from the road because it lies hidden in a deep basin surrounded by rolling, grass- and sagebrush-covered hills. It is south of the 9583-foot Druid Peak and more than 1 mile southwest of Soda Butte. There is a large vehicle turnout with a Montana bison wildlife exhibit on the south side of the highway. You can park at the turnout, cross the highway and hike to Foster Lake. There is no trail and, though it is an easy hike, you should have the Abiathar Peak 15-minute topographic map and a compass to know just where Foster Lake is located.

Because it is hidden from view and has no fish, Foster Lake is seldom visited. A trip to the lake is a pleasant experience, however, because of Foster's quiet, undisturbed setting and the beautiful views of the Lamar Valley and the surrounding cliffs and peaks. There are numerous game trails around the lake and several species of ducks can be seen on the lake.

Foster Lake has two water sources, an inlet on the north end, which drains a nearby meadow, and a small spring on the northwest shore. The outlet is a small stream at the southwest end that flows only during periods of high water. Neither stream is suitable for spawning.

There is no way for migrating fish to reach the lake, so Foster Lake was stocked with 2500 rainbow trout in 1931. Because of its shallow depth and severe winterkill, Foster Lake was barren again in 1932.

## ——— 77 ———
## Trout
## Lake

**Location** - Trailhead on the west side of the Northeast Entrance Highway, 17.4 miles northeast of Tower Junction

**Access** - Trout Lake Trail, .6 mile

**USGS topographic map** - Abiathar Peak, Wyoming–Montana

**Size** - 12 acres

**Depth** - Maximum 17 feet

**Elevation** - 6900 feet

**Fish types** - Rainbow trout, rainbow–cutthroat hybrid

There is no sign or trailhead marker to indicate the route to Trout Lake, but there is a vehicle turnout on the west side of the highway at the trailhead. The short trail leads to a series of switchbacks over a small, forested ridge, which is blanketed with wildflowers. The trail comes out above the south end of the lake and reveals beautiful views of the meadowy hillside that borders the north and west shores and 10,036-foot Mt. Hornaday to the north. Ducks are usually present on Trout Lake and buffalo frequent the meadows around the water. The area around the inlet on the north end, Trout Lake's main water source, is sometimes wet, but trails encircle the lake and passage is easy. The water is exceptionally clear and, although the lake is thick with underwater vegetation, you can almost always see large rainbow trout cruising near the shore. These fish are extremely difficult to catch, however.

*Trout Lake*

Between 1919 and 1950, Trout Lake was known as Fish Lake. During this period a fish hatchery operated at the lake to maintain a supply of cutthroat trout eggs, which were taken from spawners in Trout Lake and transplanted into other streams and lakes in the park. In 1934 rainbow trout were planted in the lake so that a supply of rainbow trout eggs could be maintained for planting in other park waters. From 1919 to 1934, Trout Lake was closed to fishing to protect the cutthroat and rainbow spawners. By 1942 rainbow-cutthroat hybrids appeared in the lake, and it was reopened to fishing in 1944.

# 78
## Buck
## Lake

**Location** - Near Trout Lake
**Access** - Foot trail and off-trail travel, .7 mile
**USGS topographic maps** - Abiathar Peak, Wyoming– Montana
**Size** - 5.3 acres
**Depth** - Maximum 37 feet
**Elevation** - 6950 feet
**Fish type** - None

Buck Lake is only about .25 mile from the highway. If you have a compass, the Abiathar Peak 15-minute topographic map and don't mind a little bushwhacking, you can get there quickly. On the other hand, it is longer but easier to start at the Trout Lake trailhead and hike the .6 mile to Trout Lake on a steep but well-defined trail. From Trout Lake you walk northeast another .1 mile to Buck Lake. You should still have a compass and topo map to know exactly where you are and

*Buck Lake*

to ensure that you're headed in the right direction. It's about a 5-minute hike from Trout Lake to Buck Lake.

Buck Lake lies in a small basin surrounded by steep, tree-covered hillsides. Its water supply comes from a small stream that flows out of nearby Shrimp Lake. There is no permanent outlet stream, but during periods of high water an outlet flow appears at the northeast corner of the lake.

Buck Lake was known for its large cutthroats: there have been reports of 5-pound trout taken from the lake. Records show that Buck Lake was stocked with 3000 cutthroats in 1931 and that spawning trout weighing from 2 to 4 and one-half pounds were trapped in 1947. Records also indicate that trout were taken from the lake in 1965, but the population has dwindled substantially since that time.

The reason for the apparent demise of the trout population in Buck Lake is its limited spawning habitat. Although good spawning habitat exists in the inlet stream, the extreme gradient of the stream entering Buck Lake limits spawning migrations.

# 79
# Shrimp Lake

**Location** - Near Trout Lake

**Access** - Foot trail and off-trail travel, .8 mile

**USGS topographic map** - Abiathar Peak, Wyoming–Montana

**Size** - 1 acre

**Depth** - Maximum 19 feet

**Elevation** - 7080 feet

**Fish type** - None

Little Shrimp Lake is seldom visited. Although it's close to the highway, it's difficult to reach. And once you are there, it hasn't much to offer—except that it might have possibilities for wildlife viewing in a very secluded setting.

To reach Shrimp Lake, start at the Trout Lake trailhead and hike the .6 mile to Trout Lake. From there, using a compass and the Abiathar Peak 15-minute topographic map, set

*Algae covers Shrimp Lake by mid-summer*

off cross-country for the remaining .2 mile north to Shrimp Lake.

Another way of getting to Shrimp Lake would be to hike to Trout Lake, then to Buck Lake and follow Buck Lake's inlet upstream to Shrimp Lake. In either case, the route is rough going and you'll have to climb through dense woods with heavy downfall.

Shrimp Lake lies in a small, circular basin surrounded by dense forest. This is a pretty little lake, except during mid-summer, when algae and duckweed form large green-brown mats on the surface of the water. The lake's inlet and main water supply comes from a small stream that flows from Trout Lake's inlet stream. The outlet, on the northeast end, flows for about .2 mile before emptying into Buck Lake.

From all appearances, Shrimp Lake should be able to sustain a fish population. Although spawning habitat is limited, it does exist. The water temperature, the rate of the water's inflow-outflow exchange, the depth and natural food sources are all what they should be to provide a suitable fishery. Cutthroat fry were stocked in the lake in 1930 and seemed to do quite well for a number of years. Shrimp Lake even produced at one time exceptionally large cutthroat trout. However, due

*Moose*

to possible winterkill, limited spawning habitat and the abundance of aquatic vegetation (which might create a low dissolved oxygen content in the water and cause summerkill), the lake defied its appearance and returned to its original barren state.

# OTHER LAKES TO EXPLORE

## 80
### Crevice Lake

**Location** - Near the Yellowstone River

**Access** - Blacktail Creek Trail, 4 miles

**USGS topographic maps** - Gardiner, Montana; Mammoth, Wyoming–Montana

**Size** - 16 acres

**Depth** - Average 58 feet, maximum 98 feet

**Elevation** - 5560 feet

**Fish type** - None

## 81
### Geode Lake

**Location** - South of the Yellowstone River near Black Canyon of the Yellowstone, unnamed on topographic maps

**Access** - Off-trail travel, approximately 1.3 miles north of the Mammoth–Tower Highway

**USGS topographic map** - Tower Junction, Wyoming–Montana

**Size** - 13 acres

**Depth** - Average 4 feet, maximum 11 feet

**Elevation** - 5960 feet

**Fish type** - None

*Bull elk*

# Mirror Plateau Region

**OTHER LAKES TO EXPLORE**

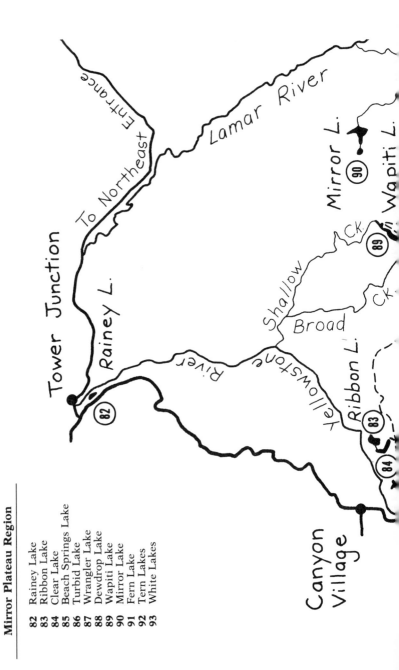

**Mirror Plateau Region**

82  Rainey Lake
83  Ribbon Lake
84  Clear Lake
85  Beach Springs Lake
86  Turbid Lake
87  Wrangler Lake
88  Dewdrop Lake
89  Wapiti Lake
90  Mirror Lake
91  Fern Lake
92  Tern Lakes
93  White Lakes

Tower Junction

To Northeast Entrance

Lamar River

Rainey L.

Mirror L.

⑨⓪

⑧⑨ CK.

Wapiti L.

Shallow

Broad

Yellowstone River

Ribbon L.

CK.

⑧②

⑧③

⑧④

Canyon Village

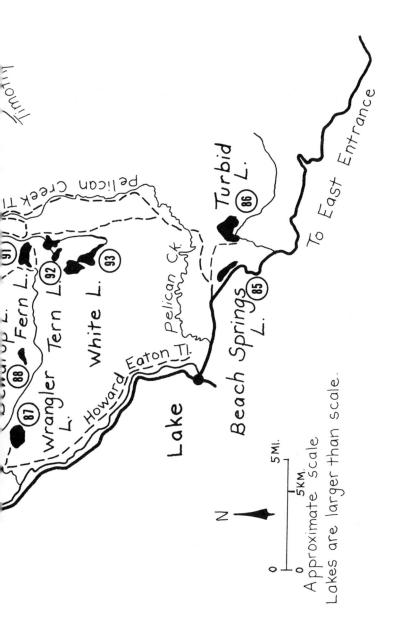

Timothy

Pelican Creek Tl.

Pelican Creek Tl.

Fern L.

Bechler L.

88

91

92

Wrangler Tern L.

93

White L.

87

Pelican Ck.

Howard Eaton Tl.

Lake

Turbid L.

86

Beach Springs L.

85

To East Entrance

N

0

0

5 MI.

5 KM.

Approximate scale
Lakes are larger than scale.

## 82
### Rainey Lake

**Location** - On the east side of the Tower–Canyon Village Highway, 1.5 miles south of Tower Falls

**Access** - On the highway

**USGS topographic map** - Tower Junction, Wyoming–Montana

**Size** - Approximately 1 acre

**Depth** - Unsurveyed, generally shallow

**Elevation** - 6360 feet

**Fish type** - None

Rainey Lake is a small, oval-shaped lake at the base of Bumpus Butte. There is no visible inlet or outlet stream. Although the lake is fed by snowmelt during spring runoff, there may also be underground springs that supply Rainey with water because the south end of the lake is marshy and swamplike and the small lake doesn't dry up during the summer. With no fish and no place to stop, this roadside lake gets few visitors.

## 83
### Ribbon Lake

**Location** - Near the Grand Canyon of the Yellowstone

**Access** - Foot trail, 2 miles

**USGS topographic map** - Canyon Village, Wyoming

**Size** - 11 acres

**Depth** - Maximum 19 feet

**Elevation** - 7820 feet

**Fish type** - Rainbow trout

The short hike to Ribbon Lake is one of the prettiest and most spectacular in Yellowstone. The trail begins at Artist Point, just south of Canyon Village, and follows along the rim of the Grand Canyon of the Yellowstone for half a mile before turning south and entering the forest. The view of the canyon

*Rainey Lake*

walls and the Yellowstone River below is breathtaking, especially at sunrise and sunset, when the hues of yellow, orange and red (a result of the oxidation of iron compounds in the rhyolite cliffs) are at their peak. Shortly after turning and entering the forest, you will pass a small, lilypad-covered pond on your right. Just past the pond the trail will fork. The left fork will take you the remaining 1.3 miles to Ribbon Lake. To the right Clear Lake is .5 mile and the Artist Point Road and

*Ribbon Lake*

trailhead across from the parking.area at Uncle Tom's Cabin
is 2 miles. Just a 100 yards or so from this trail junction, to
the right toward Clear Lake, is a thermal area with fumaroles, hot springs and boiling mud pots.

Ribbon Lake is actually 2 lakes joined by a short, narrow
channel a foot or so deep. When you first come upon the lake,
to your right and slightly below the trail, you will be at the
smaller lake and the larger lake will be visible in the background. The smaller lake, only about 3 feet deep, is covered
with yellow pond lilies, surrounded by sedge meadows and is
difficult to get around without getting wet. The larger lake
too is surrounded by meadows and is wet and somewhat
marshy close to the lake. Most of the larger lake is ringed with
yellow pond lilies. They grow close to shore and make fishing
for the small rainbow trout in this lake rather difficult.

Groundwater seepage and small springs contribute to the

lake's water supply, although Surface Creek, flowing into the south end, is the primary source of Ribbon Lake's water. The outlet stream flows from the north end for about 600 feet before falling over Silver Cord Cascade, on the rim of the Grand Canyon of the Yellowstone, 1300 feet into the Yellowstone River. This is a magnificent sight and hikers will find it worth their while to continue on the trail just a short distance past Ribbon Lake to Silver Cord Cascade.

Originally, Ribbon Lake was barren. Rainbow trout were planted in the lake, but there are no records to document who planted them or when.

## 84
## Clear Lake

**Location** - Near the Grand Canyon of the Yellowstone
**Access** - Foot trail, 1.5 miles
**USGS topographic map** - Canyon Village, Wyoming
**Size** - Approximately 3 acres
**Depth** - Unsurveyed
**Elevation** - 7760 feet
**Fish type** - None

*Clear Lake*

*Grand Canyon of the Yellowstone near Ribbon Lake Trail*

There are actually 2 trails that will lead you to Clear Lake, both of them about 1.5 miles to the lake. One starts from the vehicle parking area on the south side of the Artist Point Road, .2 mile from the Canyon Highway turnoff. At first this trail climbs slightly, crossing a large, grassy meadow. After about a half mile, hikers will turn left at the trail junction and continue 1 mile to Clear Lake. The second trail, the Ribbon Lake Trail, begins at Artist Point and follows along the rim of the Grand Canyon of the Yellowstone, which offers spectacular views into the canyon. After a half mile along the canyon rim, the trail will turn south, into the forest and you will soon pass a small, lily pad-covered pond on your right. Just past the pond the trail will fork. To the right is Clear Lake, .5 mile. If you stop and listen, just past the trail junction, you should be able to hear the bubbling mud pot that you will soon see to the left of the trail. This small thermal area has hot springs, fumaroles and boiling mud pots.

Small and quite pretty, spring-fed Clear Lake is enjoyable to visit and interesting to explore because of the delicate features surrounding the lake. It lies in a circular basin completely surrounded by forest on the edge of a thermal area. The clear, green water of Clear Lake is cool, even though it gives the impression that it's hot, because of the adjacent thermal area, dead trees and downfalls around its beachlike shoreline. Spring activity surrounds the lake basin and the water bubbles up, fountain-like, in several areas in the lake. The most active display is in the middle of the lake.

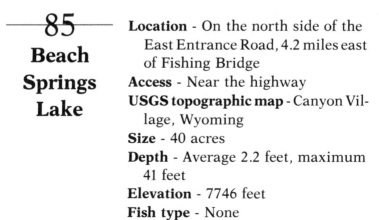

## 85
## Beach Springs Lake

**Location** - On the north side of the East Entrance Road, 4.2 miles east of Fishing Bridge

**Access** - Near the highway

**USGS topographic map** - Canyon Village, Wyoming

**Size** - 40 acres

**Depth** - Average 2.2 feet, maximum 41 feet

**Elevation** - 7746 feet

**Fish type** - None

Beach Springs Lake is one of those lakes you might ordinarily pass by since it is directly across the highway from Yellowstone Lake's Mary Bay. It lies in a flat open area about 100 yards off the highway and is only partly visible. There is a steep, grass- and tree-covered hillside directly across from the lake and a small thermal area at its western end. It is an easy walk to the lake across a sage-covered, sandy flat.

Beach Springs Lake's water originates in underground springs. There is an additional spring that flows to the lake from the thermal area on the west end. There is no outlet stream.

Due to the lack of spawning habitat, there are no trout in Beach Springs Lake and there are no records to indicate that it has ever been stocked.

Beach Springs Lake almost always has a variety of wildlife on and around it. Because of its somewhat marshy environment and its close proximity to Yellowstone Lake, it is an excellent area to see and photograph Canada geese, trumpeter swans, western grebes, ospreys, great blue herons and a variety of ducks. It is also one of the few areas in Yellowstone where you can sometimes see a grizzly bear from the safety of your car.

# 86
# Turbid Lake

**Location** - Trailhead .3 mile from the turnoff of East Entrance Highway, 3 miles east of Fish Bridge

**Access** - Turbid Lake Trail, 3 miles

**USGS topographic map** - Canyon Village, Wyoming

**Size** - 143 acres

**Depth** - Average 17 feet, maximum 125 feet

**Elevation** - 7837 feet

**Fish type** - None

Across from Indian Pond, 3 miles east of Fishing Bridge, a dirt road will angle off the north side of the highway and dead end .3 mile at the trailhead to Turbid Lake. The hike to the lake is

*Grizzly with radio collar at Beach Springs Lake*

*Turbid Lake*

an easy one, on an old service road, across large meadows and through dense forest. The trail comes out on the west side of Turbid Lake and continues above the southwestern shore for .3 mile before leaving the lake and continuing south. It eventually joins the East Entrance Highway, about 2 miles west of Yellowstone Lake.

Elk, moose, buffalo and coyotes spend most of the summer feeding in this part of the Pelican Valley and the possibility of seeing any or all of them is good. So is the possibility of seeing a bear. This is a high bear-use area and grizzlies are often seen roaming this part of the valley. This is a good hike if you want to see a variety of wildlife, but one that you should not take alone. If you do go alone, remain alert and make plenty of noise.

Turbid Lake was named in 1878 by members of the Hayden Expedition. Underwater springs in the lake bubble constantly, causing the turbidity and congealed-looking, murky, tan waters that lap and foam at its shores. Turbid Lake is the most acidic lake in Yellowstone. Trees that have taken root too close to the lake stand dying or dead. At first glance the lake seems unfriendly and forbidding, as if nothing could survive in so harsh an environment. However, spending time to explore the area around the lake, walking along the south and western shoreline among bubbling springs and sulfurous gases hissing from the earth is like going back in time to the dawn of creation. On closer inspection, Turbid Lake becomes a fascinating lake to visit.

A mixed forest of lodgepole pine, spruce and fir surrounds most of the lake basin and borders its shores on the west, southwest and a small portion of the south end. The meadowy hillside on the north end is covered with wildflowers and offers a good vantage point for viewing the entire basin. Turbid Lake lies above a large mud flat that extends from the north end, near the Sedge Creek inlet, most of the way around the east side. It is here on the north end, near Sedge Creek, that you can almost always see large concentrations of Canada geese.

The water supply to Turbid Lake comes from seeps all around the lake and from two inlet streams, Sedge Creek on the northeast and Bear Creek on the south. Above the lake, both Sedge and Bear creeks contain small, native cutthroat trout. The outlet stream, Sedge Creek, flows from the west side of the lake for about 2 miles before emptying into Yellowstone Lake's Sedge Bay.

# OTHER LAKES TO EXPLORE

## —— 87 ——
## Wrangler Lake

**Location** - Near the Grand Canyon of the Yellowstone, about 2 miles southeast of Artist Point

**Access** - Wrangler Lake Trail, 3 miles

**USGS topographic map** - Canyon Village, Wyoming

**Size** - 35 acres

**Depth** - Average 16 feet, maximum
    33 feet
**Elevation** - 7860 feet
**Fish type** - None

## 88
## Dewdrop
## Lake

**Location** - Southeast of Artist Point
    at the headwaters of Bog Creek
**Access** - Off-trail travel, 6 miles
**USGS topographic map** - Canyon Village, Wyoming
**Size** - 9 acres
**Depth** - Average 12 feet, maximum
    25 feet
**Elevation** - 8139 feet
**Fish type** - None

*Cutleaf daisies*

## 89
## Wapiti Lake

**Location** - North of Pelican Valley and northeast of Fern Lake

**Access** - Wapiti Lake Trail, 15 miles; Astringent Creek–Broad Creek Trail to Wapiti Lake Trail, 14 miles

**USGS topographic map** - Canyon Village, Wyoming

**Size** - 11 acres

**Depth** - Average 6 feet, maximum 15 feet

**Elevation** - 8440 feet

**Fish type** - None

## 90
## Mirror Lake

**Location** - Southeast of Artist Point

**Access** - Off-trail travel, approximately 16 miles east of Canyon Village

**USGS topographic map** - Pelican Cone, Wyoming

**Size** - 7 acres

**Depth** - Average 6 feet, maximum 13 feet

**Elevation** - 8800 feet

**Fish type** - None

## 91
## Fern Lake

**Location** - North of Pelican Valley

**Access** - Pelican Creek Trail to Astringent Creek–Broad Creek Trail to Fern Lake Trail, 11.5 miles

**USGS topographic map** - Canyon Village, Wyoming

**Size** - 90 acres

**Depth** - Average 13 feet, maximum 25 feet

**Elevation** - 8245 feet
**Fish type** - Cutthroat trout

## 92
## Tern Lakes

**Location** - North of the Pelican Valley between White and Fern lakes
**Access** - Astringent Creek–Broad Creek Trail from Pelican Valley Trailhead, 9.5 miles
**USGS topographic map** - Canyon Village, Wyoming
**Sizes** - East Tern Lake 54 acres, West Tern Lake 32 acres
**Depths** - East Tern Lake average 1 foot, maximum 3 feet; West Tern Lake average 5 feet, maximum 9 feet
**Elevation** - 8240 feet
**Fish type** - None

## 93
## White Lakes

**Location** - North of Pelican Valley at the headwaters of Broad Creek
**Access** - Astringent Creek–Broad Creek Trail from the Pelican Valley Trailhead, 8.5 miles
**USGS topographic map** - Canyon Village, Wyoming
**Sizes** - North White Lake 74 acres, South White Lake 96 acres
**Depths** - North White Lake average 22 feet, maximum 50 feet; South White Lake average 7 feet, maximum 22 feet
**Elevation** - 8218 feet
**Fish type** - Cutthroat trout

*Backcountry closure sign*

# APPENDIX A

## LAKE ACCESS AND DISTANCES

### Lakes on the highway

These lakes are located along the highway and most have vehicle turnouts or parking areas at or near the lake.

| | |
|---|---|
| Beaver Lake | Phantom Lake |
| Divide Lake | Rainey Lake |
| Eleanor Lake | Scaup Lake |
| Floating Island Lake | Sylvan Lake |
| Isa Lake | Yellowstone Lake |
| Lewis Lake | |

### Lakes near the highway

These lakes have highway access and most can be seen from the road. You will have to walk from 100 to 500 feet to reach them and the trail may not be maintained.

| | |
|---|---|
| Beach Springs Lake | Nymph Lake |
| Blacktail Pond | Swan Lake |
| Duck Lake | North Twin Lake |
| Indian Pond | South Twin Lake |
| Lower Basin Lake | |

*Buffalo crossing the Yellowstone River in Hayden valley*

# Lakes accessible by gravel or dirt road

These lakes can be driven to, but on gravel or dirt roads off the main highways.

Feather Lake
Goose Lake

Joffe Lake

# Lakes accessible by day hikes (shortest route noted)

| .1 to .5 mile | | .6 to .9 mile | |
|---|---|---|---|
| Slide Lakes | .1 | Trout Lake | .6 |
| Ice Lake | .2 | Buck Lake | .7 |
| Foster Lake | .3 | Obsidian Lake | .7 |
| Trumpeter Lakes | .3 | Shrimp Lake | .8 |
| Harlequin Lake | .4 | | |
| Lost Lake | .5 | | |

| 1 to 2 miles | | 2 to 3 miles | |
|---|---|---|---|
| Tanager Lake | 1 | Beula Lake | 2.5 |
| Clear Lake | 1.5 | Cascade Lake | 2.5 |
| Lake of the Woods | 1.5 | Riddle Lake | 2.5 |
| Grizzly Lake | 1.8 | Grebe Lake | 3 |
| Ribbon Lake | 2 | Hering Lake | 3 |
| | | Lilypad Lake | 3 |
| | | McBride Lake | 3 |
| | | Turbid Lake | 3 |

| Over 3 miles | |
|---|---|
| Mallard Lake | 3.3 |
| Shoshone Lake | 4.5 |
| Wolf Lake | 4 |

## Other Lakes to Explore (shortest route noted)

| Lake | Miles | Cross Country (CC) or Foot Trail (FT) |
|------|-------|----------------------------------------|
| Alder Lake | .1 | CC |
| Pocket Lake | 1.1 | CC |
| Geode Lake | 1.3 | CC |
| Robinson Lake | 2 | FT |
| South Boundary Lake | 2 | FT |
| Mammoth Beaver Ponds | 2.5 | FT |
| Rainbow Lakes | 2.5 | FT |
| Forest Lake | 2.8 | FT & CC |
| Wrangler Lake | 3 | FT |
| DeLacy Lakes | 3.5 | CC |
| Aster Lake | 4 | CC |
| Crevice Lake | 4 | FT |
| Cygnet Lakes | 4 | unmaintained FT |
| Dryad Lake | 4 | FT & CC |
| Winegar Lake | 4 | FT |
| Fawn Lake | 5 | FT |
| Beach Lake | 5.5 | FT |
| Delusion Lake | 5.5 | CC |
| Cache Lake | 6 | FT |
| Dewdrop Lake | 6 | FT & CC |
| Glade Lake | 6.8 | CC |
| Crescent Lake | 7 | FT |
| Summit Lake | 7.5 | FT |
| Heart Lake | 8 | FT |
| Shelf Lake | 8 | FT |
| Wyodaho Lake | 8 | FT & CC |
| Ranger Lake | 8.25 | FT & CC |
| Crag Lake | 8.5 | FT & CC |
| White Lakes | 8.5 | FT |
| High Lake | 9 | FT |
| Trilobite Lake | 9 | FT |
| Tern Lakes | 9.5 | FT |
| Gallatin Lake | 10 | FT & CC |

*Trumpeter swan*

*Evidence of active beavers at Lost Lake*

| Lake | Miles | Cross Country (CC) or Foot Trail (FT) |
|------|-------|---------------------------------------|
| Basin Creek Lake | 11 | FT |
| Mary Lake | 11 | FT |
| Sportsman Lake | 11 | FT |
| Fern Lake | 11.5 | FT |
| Sheridan Lake | 12 | FT |
| Wapiti Lake | 14 | FT |
| Outlet Lake | 15 | FT |
| Buffalo Lake | 16 | FT |
| Mirror Lake | 16 | CC |
| Mariposa Lake | 28 | FT |
| Trail Lake | 28 | FT |

# APPENDIX B

## LAKES WITH SPORT FISH

| | |
|---|---|
| Alder Lake | Cutthroat trout |
| Basin Creek Lake | Cutthroat trout |
| Beaver Lake | Brook trout |
| Beula Lake | Cutthroat trout |
| Blacktail Pond | Cutthroat, brook trout |
| Cascade Lake | Cutthroat trout, grayling |
| Eleanor Lake | Cutthroat trout |
| Fawn Lake | Brook trout |
| Fern Lake | Cutthroat trout |
| Goose Lake | Rainbow trout |
| Grebe Lake | Rainbow trout, grayling |
| Grizzly Lake | Brook trout |
| Heart Lake | Cutthroat, lake trout |
| Hering Lake | Cutthroat trout |
| High Lake | Cutthroat trout |
| Indian Pond | Cutthroat trout |
| Joffe Lake | Brook trout |
| Lewis Lake | Brown, lake and brook trout |
| Mariposa Lake | Cutthroat trout, rainbow – cutthroat hybrids |

*Yellow pond lily*

| | |
|---|---|
| McBride Lake | Cutthroat trout |
| Outlet Lake | Cutthroat trout |
| Pocket Lake | Cutthroat trout |
| Ranger Lake | Rainbow trout |
| Ribbon Lake | Rainbow trout |
| Riddle Lake | Cutthroat trout |
| Sheridan Lake | Cutthroat trout |
| Shoshone Lake | Brown, lake and brook trout |
| Slide Lake (Little) | Rainbow trout |
| Sportsman Lake | Cutthroat trout |
| Sylvan Lake | Cutthroat trout |
| Trail Lake | Cutthroat trout |
| Trilobite Lake | Brook trout |
| Trout Lake | Rainbow trout, rainbow–cutthroat hybrid |
| White Lakes | Cutthroat trout |
| Wolf Lake | Rainbow trout, grayling |
| Yellowstone Lake | Cutthroat trout |

# APPENDIX C

## LAKES WITHOUT SPORT FISH

| | |
|---|---|
| Aster Lake | Feather Lake |
| Beach Lake | Floating Island Lake |
| Beach Springs Lake | Forest Lake |
| Buck Lake | Foster Lake |
| Buffalo Lake | Gallatin Lake |
| Cache Lake | Geode Lake |
| Clear Lake | Glade Lake |
| Crag Lake | Harlequin Lake |
| Crescent Lake | Ice Lake |
| Crevice Lake | Isa Lake |
| Cygnet Lakes | Lake of the Woods |
| DeLacy Lakes | Lilypad Lake |
| Delusion Lake | Lost Lake |
| Dewdrop Lake | Lower Basin Lake |
| Divide Lake | Mallard Lake |
| Dryad Lake | Mammoth Beaver Ponds |
| Duck Lake | Mary Lake |

Mirror Lake
North Twin Lake
Nymph Lake
Obsidian Lake
Phantom Lake
Rainbow Lakes
Rainey Lake
Robinson Lake
Scaup Lake
Shelf Lake
Shrimp Lake
Slide Lake (Big)

South Boundary Lake
South Twin Lake
Summit Lake
Swan Lake
Tanager Lake
Tern Lakes
Trumpeter Lakes
Turbid Lake
Wapiti Lake
Winegar Lake
Wrangler Lake
Wyodaho Lake

*Trailhead sign to Turbid Lake trailhead*

# INDEX

AUTHOR STEVE PIERCE, a Durango, Colorado resident, fell in love with Yellowstone National Park on his first visit, in 1956. He has returned almost every year since, to hike, fish, and explore the vast wild areas of the Park. He began researching the Park's lakes in the early 1970s, mostly for his own satisfaction. In order to record all he'd discovered about the lakes—their formation, their water sources, their evolution during modern times, their fisheries history and potential—he began writing this book in 1985. With literally hundreds more lakes out there awaiting study and recording, Pierce's continuing research is likely to occupy his spare time for years to come.

Born in California and reared in Texas, Pierce followed a business degree from the University of Houston with a career as a freelance photographer-writer. His work has taken him to many exotic vacation areas in the western hemisphere, resulting in articles and photos in numerous travel magazines. However, he and his family (wife Marilyn and two children) share a love of skiing, hiking and backpacking that has resulted in a home base in the mountains of Colorado since 1975. Pierce is now at work on his second book.